25 Key Topics in Human Resources

Essential revision for coursework and examinations

Chris Sivewright

Principal, The Oxford School of Learning

www.**studymates**.co.uk

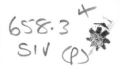

25 Key Topics in Human Resources

Essential revision for coursework and examinations

Studymates

Many other titles in preparation

Contents

List of illustrations

Preface

This guide has been designed to help all those studying Human Resources for A-levels, professional examinations or during their first year at university. Throughout this book the emphasis is on providing ideas and material to interest and absorb you – without overwhelming you with extraneous factual information. Discussion topics and practical assignments are very much a feature of the Studymates series and they have all been carefully designed to help you learn.

Twenty years ago, the Business Studies market was underresourced. Today there is a mass of academic material, but in it the purpose of education is often overlooked. Teaching is the art of bringing about learning. The key purpose of this guide is to encourage you to *discuss* and to *think* and thereby truly learn – not just learn facts for their own sake.

The book begins with a discussion of the meaning of Human Resource Management. Further topics include motivation, trade unions and stress. Wherever possible practical, current examples (1999) are given. It is recognised that to some extent these examples will date – but that is true of all textbooks. The law in this book – UK and European – is current as of late 1999.

Each chapter has been kept to approximately 1,200 words – long enough to include definitions, examples and brief discussion (with scope for further work), but also short enough to be read in about twenty minutes. The book has been designed not to wear you out, but to stimulate and help you learn – speedily and surely. Many of the 'practical assignments' at the end of each chapter depend on the internet being available, as a resource for information, discussion and analysis. Some chapters suggest that the reader turns to his/her place of study for the information. After all schools, colleges and universities – in common with all organisations – employ people. Wherever there are people, there are needs and these needs often conflict. Sometimes the needs are not met and this is where motivation is insufficient.

No one publication can hope to be a definitive guide to human resources. But if reading this book has stimulated you to think more deeply about this fascinating subject, then its goal has been achieved. Your new awareness of the many challenging issues in human resource management should help you make a very worthwhile contribution in the modern workplace, whatever your chosen career path may be.

Chris Sivewright
chrissivewright@studymates.co.uk

1

What is Human Resource Management?

One-minute summary – Human resource management is a much
broader term than just simply 'personnel management'. It
encompasses the development of workers within a team that
contributes towards the business's objectives. Accordingly, the
Human Resources Management department incorporates the
Personnel department functions and develops them. The role of
HRM is to enable workers to contribute to their maximum
efficiency towards the objectives of the business. In order to do
that, a variety of functions are incorporated within the overall
functions of the Human Resources Manager. In this chapter we
will discuss:

▶ definitions
▶ the objectives of human resource management
▶ human resource management functions

Definitions

▶ *Key definition* – 'Human Resource Management concerns the
 human side of the management of enterprises and employees
 relations with the firms ... ' Source: Graham & Bennett, *Human
 Resource Management* (7th edition).

As workers become more empowered, it is argued, there is less
need for the management of relationships. As each worker
becomes more responsible for their own quality of output, then
there is less for the Personnel department to do.
 This empowerment is not just the HRM showing his
acquiescence to the needs of the workers as they struggle against
the boredom of work. Rather it is the constant pressure to cut costs,

improve quality and productivity. With a reduction in the need for supervision there is thus less need for supervisors – and hence there will be a cut in wage costs.

With the reduction in middle managers there has been a shift in power, a disempowerment away from the Human Resources professionals and towards the line managers. Policy-related issues will go before the directors, but day to day decisions may be taken by the team leaders of autonomous work groups.

The objectives of HRM

1. As with all departments, the overall role of the Human Resource Department is to contribute towards the company objectives.

2. 'The bottom line in Human Resource Management is profitability and financial performance.' (Source: Fernie & Metcalfe, London School of Economics.)

3. 'To help a company achieve its business strategy by maximising the performance of its employees. Better management-employee relations are not necessarily a sign of success. The assumed validity of the notion of management-employee relations is indicative of the continued prevalence of command-control management style. Individuals empower themselves when they recognise the self-interest in the job they are performing. Individuals do not take a job just to further the business goals of the company – they take a job to further their personal GOALS. Only when the two coincide can a company hope to maximise the commitment of its people and thus facilitate the attainment of its business objectives.' (Source: Tom Barry, Managing Director, Blessing/White Performance Improvement, Windsor.)

HRM functions

Motivation
Not only must workers work as hard as possible, but they should

also be happy in their work. Happiness often stems from security; without this security, ill health will often result. According to a report by the Joseph Rowntree Foundation (*Job Insecurity and Work Intensification*, July 1999), workers' fears of losing their jobs are at their highest level since the Second World War, and the stress is taking its toll on their physical well-being.

According to the Rowntree study, two-thirds of employees said they regularly worked overtime. Thirty per cent of full-time male employees claimed they worked more than 48 hours a week. The cause of the stress was staff cutbacks. The same amount of work being done by fewer people leads to extra stress.

The report found that those admitting to the greatest feelings of insecurity were five times more likely to be in poor health. Supportive relationships between managers and staff relieve the pressure which will in turn lead to better health. The Human Resources function in this case would not just be to try and motivate the workers, but also to encourage Directors and below to be supportive of their staff. Such support would include improved communication and greater transparency in management decisions.

Training and education of the workforce
Training will increase the status of the workers as well as their self-esteem. Universities are now in competition with each other as A-level passes continue to rise. With the competition for standards come also a variety of courses.

In 1997 Loughborough University launched a BSc in Retail Automotive Management. The course was designed for car salesmen; the press dubbed it as the 'Arthur Daley Degree in Duping'.

The Course Director when interviewed stated: 'Every other aspect of the retail trade has become a highly professional discipline and what we are doing is responding to the needs of the market. Some car dealerships now employ more than 200 people and skills such as human resource management and marketing are vitally important.

The degree is sponsored by Ford. They consulted with their own Human Resources Department about the course content, and the need for such a qualification. Thus, the Human Resources function here has extended beyond just helping the existing work force, to providing advice for external training courses.

A Masters degree has also been proposed. Since Ford already sponsors a chair at Loughborough, it is not out of the question that there could soon be a Professor of Car Dealing.

Dealing with employee grievances

If an employee is unhappy with his or her working life, such unhappiness may manifest itself in poor quality work. When taking disciplinary action against such workers, the employer must take great care must be taken that all disciplinary matters follow procedure – and that allegations made are supported.

In July 1996, a typing error cost a Labour council dearly. David Morgan, a council caretaker, was paid undisclosed libel damages by a Labour council over a misprint, which suggested that he was racist. A letter from the Human Resources Manager stated that Mr Morgan was sacked because he could not get on with 'black caretakers'. The High Court was told that Mr Melling had meant to write 'block caretakers'.

The letter said: 'He could not get on with staff such as black caretakers and that he improperly removed, disseminated and falsified pages from a council notebook.' Counsel for Mr Morgan told the court that even allowing for the misprint, the first allegation had been withdrawn by the council, while its own inquiry had found nothing improper in the second. Both Mr Melling and the council denied implying racism, saying the allegations were published inadvertently and in good faith. They agreed to pay damages, believed to be £6,000, and costs.

Evaluation of potential employees

With the widening of the Personnel Manager's function to that of Human Resource Manager, greater financial evaluation of potential staff takes place before recruitment. To meet this need, a new service was launched by Arthur Anderson, the management consultancy firm.

In 1996 Anderson set up a 'Human Capital Services' division to advise on executive compensation, reward strategies, human resource management, share schemes, pensions and profits-related pay. The head of the division is Mr Friedman, who said: 'Many organisations say their people are their most important asset, yet they fail to measure the value they bring. Ultimately businesses can only sustain a competitive advantage through continual investment in their people. However, it is vital that businesses know what advantages and returns this expenditure really brings. Andersen would help companies measure and justify their investment in people by objectively calculating its payback using rigorous, analytical and strategic skills.'

Tutorial

Progress questions
1. What is Human Resource Management?
2. State one function of the HRM department.
3. What are the other departments in a business?

Discussion point
According to David Dyer, Chief Examiner for Cambridge Modular, the ' ... HRM approach is the intention to emphasise a total strategy related to a firms most valued resource ... ' Have other departments – Production, Marketing, Finance – evolved as the Personnel function has?

Practical assignment
'Our own work suggests a dichotomy. HRM appears to be associated with better economic outcomes in the workplace – higher productivity and better performance on the jobs front – but worse industrial relations outcomes – higher number of resignations, higher absenteeism and less good relations between management and employees ... ' (Source: Fernie & Metcalf). Suggest possible reasons for this dichotomy.

Study/revision tip
Make sure you can list all the main functions of an HRM department.

2

Attitude & Perception

One-minute summary – An attitude is made up of thought, feelings and behaviour. Correct assessment of the attitude of the employees will enable a suitable training programme to be devised, suitable motivation schemes to be applied and the most suitable applicants for posts being recruited. In order to establish the attitudes of the workforce, surveys may be carried out. When workers are asked to voice their opinions, though, it is vital that such opinions are at least acknowledged and, preferably, acted on. In this chapter we will discuss:

► attitude
► the attitude survey
► perception
► cross-training

Attitude

An attitude has three components:

1. thinking
2. feelings
3. behaviour.

It is these three elements that combine to determine how we are going to behave. How a person behaves at work is a product of inherent characteristics, internal events (at work) and external events (outside of work).

Inherent characteristics
These include:

1. character – introvert/extrovert
2. achiever – high/low
3. determination/willpower
4. risk-taking/aversion to risk.

Internal events
Internal events are those taking place at the workplace. They could include:

1. attitude of the supervisor
2. attitudes of colleagues
3. company policy
4. working conditions
5. social aspects – for example personality clashes with workers/ between workers.

External events
External events are those taking place outside the place of work. They could include:

1. a rise in interest rates (thus causing people with mortgages extra financial hardship)

2. a change in the level of income tax

3. a relaxation of planning rules leading to a new motorway being built outside your house!

Planning changes
If change is planned, then it is important that the employer can assess the likely responses. Typical changes include:

(a) change in working hours/practices
(b) relocation
(c) change of product
(d) change of process
(e) change of pay arrangements
(f) change in ownership.

The attitude survey

In order to assess the attitude of employees a survey may be carried out. For example, questions may be asked about the employees' attitude to the new canteen, the change (proposed change) in working practices, and the employees' satisfaction with the job/supervisor/company.

This exercise in employee consultation can go wrong, though. It is one thing to ask for an opinion – quite another to act in accordance with that opinion. In some cases the survey may even be a demotivator and it would be better not to have conducted it in the first place.

Potential negative aspects
The survey may have negative effects if:

(a) No action is taken on the general results.

(b) The results are not published.

(c) Other actions (not recommended) are taken that actually worsen the situation.

(d) The survey asks ambiguous questions that merely confirm the workers' views that management are incompetent.

(e) There is no clear idea as to what to do with the results. No budget has been allocated.

(f) The costs of the survey means that certain things have to be cancelled, for example the building of a new sports hall for the workers.

(g) The completion form is long and rambling, response rate is low, and the time devoted to filling in the form must be the workers' own time.

Potential positive aspects of the survey
On the positive side, the survey may highlight genuine areas of

concern for the workforce. The workforce may be unhappy about the proposed relocation of the factory, about the new incentive scheme or even about the new product range. Taking the incentive scheme as an example, management may decide to temporarily shelve the scheme and set up a working party to examine different ways to reward the workers without greatly increasing costs.

Possible results from a survey

The Royal Mail carried out an attitude survey among its 180,000 employees. The results showed that morale was low as a result of:

1. uncertainty over the possibility of future privatisation

2. reorganisation of the service

3. new technology

4. government policy on pay.

Perception

Accurate perception of the workforce is also important.

1. Promoting a person unable to take stress to a position that raises his profile, may lead to a substandard performance.

2. Weaker workers who need training may be passed over simply because they were not the first in the queue of those who applied for extra courses.

3. Equally the actual perception of the types of training may have an effect on the success of the actual training programme.

Cross-training

As part of their preparation for the 1999 World Cup (which they eventually won) the Australian Institute of Sport hired specialists from a variety of other sports disciplines to help train their rugby players. At first glance, the sports are totally mismatched:

1. A top darts player helped train lineout throwers in hand-eye co-ordination.

2. Judo experts helped train the players to throw someone when tackling and how to roll on landing and return to their feet as quickly as possible.

3. Trampolinists helped the lineout jumpers reach their maximum height.

4. A netball team lined the rugby squad against a wall and trained them to collect the ball on a bounce.

▶ *Key point* – What matters is that the training is pitched at the right level to the right audience – and at the right time. If a worker is wrongly appraised, if the attitude of the workforce is misjudged, then decisions will be made that are likely to meet with at worst hostility, and at best apathy.

Tutorial

Progress questions
1. What are the key components in 'attitude?

2. What factors affect the attitude of the workforce?

3. Why is it important for employers to be aware of changes in their employees' attitude?

Discussion points
1. The results of the Royal Mail attitude survey are shown above. Why would each of the areas shown be a cause for a lack of motivation?

2. Has the attitude of public sector employees improved or worsened under this Labour Government?

Practical assignment

Carry out an attitude survey in your school or college. Before sending round the questionnaire, consider not only the type of questions but also their form and order. How important is confidentiality? What will you do with the results?

Study and revision tips

1. Managers who disregard the feelings of the workforce risk working in isolation.

2. Without considering the workforce, conflict is likely.

3

Motivation:
The Scientific School of Management

One-minute summary – the main motivators for people today may seem commonplace but their application is based on sound empirical work. Although biographies are not required, students must still be aware of the work of motivational theorists, in particular those of the Scientific and Human Relations School of Management. The founder of the Scientific School was Frederick Taylor. In this chapter we will discuss:

▶ main motivators
▶ Scientific School of Management, incorporating the Classical School
▶ criticisms of the Scientific School of Management

Main motivators

The main motivating factors for people at work may be grouped into financial and non-financial.

Financial factors
The financial factors include:

1. basic rate of pay
2. overtime rate
3. other bonuses such as productivity schemes
4. profit sharing.

Non-financial factors
The non-financial factors include:

1. job title
2. supervisor's attitude
3. working conditions
4. praise
5. sense of achievement
6. job security
7. promotional opportunities
8. colleagues
9. degree of initiative required
10. responsibility

These motivators have their grounding in the work of the various schools of management theory.

The Scientific School of Management

The Classical School of Management incorporates the Scientific School of Management.

The Classical School
The Classical School was mainly concerned with the structure and activities of formal organisations. The main theorist was Henri Fayol. He maintained that management was a skill that could be taught. Fayol created ideas that could be applied to all areas of management and he laid down rules for the management of large organisations.
His principles included:

1. division of labour
2. centralisation
3. esprit de corps
4. unity of direction
5. unity of command
6. remuneration
7. subordination of the individual's interests to those of the firm as a whole.

The Scientific School

The father of Scientific Management was F.W. Taylor. In 1911, Taylor published his book the *Principles of Scientific Management*. In this he identified three key principles of management:

1. Each worker should have a daily task that has been clearly defined.

2. Standard conditions are needed to ensure that the task is more easily established.

3. High payment should be made for successful completion of tasks. Workers should suffer a loss when they fail to meet the standards laid down.

Key topic areas inherent in Scientific Management

1. division of labour

2. simplification, standardisation, specialisation

3. time and motion studies

4. emphasis on recruitment process and training – always seeking the 'best way' for a task to be carried out.

Criticisms of the Scientific School

Unitary-v-pluralist view

▶ *The unitary view* – The Classical School assumed there was one best way for managing a business. They took a unitary view of management and workers. This is the view that workers will support management. If the company benefits, then so will the workers. Thus they should work hard to help the company grow. If workers do not support management this must because they are militant trade unionists or have simply been misinformed about management views.

▶ *The pluralist view* – The 'unitary' view has largely been replaced by the pluralist view. The pluralist view sees employees having different views, aims and aspirations. The task of management is therefore to not only identify but to represent, co-ordinate and fulfil the aspirations of the differing parties. If workers want a pay increase, this could be paid for by an increase in productivity. Thus unit labour costs fall (helping the business become more competitive) but wages rise, so pleasing the workers.

Social and psychological factors are over-simplified

Social and psychological factors will affect motivation at the workplace. Behaviour is the product of inherited characteristics, early socialisation, the workplace environment and external factors. It would be simplistic to think that every individual will work harder because of the bonuses offered.

Treatment of labour

Division of labour may mean allocating individual workers different tasks, which they then carry out ad infinitum. Division of labour can therefore lead to boredom and also to poor quality work, high absenteeism and high labour turnover. Workers lose their autonomy and feel alienated.

The current employment scene

Despite the criticisms by many of Taylor's work, similar criticisms are made in 1999 about the modern employee. In an age when employees have more legal rights than ever before (for example regarding maternity, paternity, and equal pay) the very speed of change has lead to greater job insecurity. Consultation may be seen to slow things down but over-rapid change causes fear. Firms are increasingly customer-driven.

The growth of e-commerce via the internet has led to customers having access to ever-greater information banks. Management sees opportunities in the global market that were previously not available owing to the lack of technology. On the other hand, employees are worried about technology displacing jobs, age becoming a perceived barrier to learning, and 'initiative fatigue' has set in.

With the growth of IT, many workers now feel they are merely an adjunct to a computer. They feel a sense of disaffection as they no longer identify with the company; the gap between them and those at the 'cutting edge' running the company seems to have grown wider.

Tutorial

Progress questions
1. Name two financial factors affecting motivation in the workplace.

2. Under Taylor, how may workers be motivated?

3. What were the main criticisms of Taylor's theory?

Discussion points
Does the validity/effectiveness of Taylor's theory of motivation increase or decrease during a recession?

Practical assignments
1. Compose a questionnaire for teachers at your place of study. List ten motivational factors including status, power, working hours, pay, holidays and job satisfaction. Ask the teachers to list the factors in order of importance to them regarding their own particular job. Analyse the responses and categorise according to subject and level taught. For example, are the Science teachers motivated by the same factors that motivate those involved in Arts?

2. Research the work of Taylor, Gilbreth and Gantt. In what ways does their work overlap?

Study and revision tips
Taylor treated people as machines; thus the key is training, but the motivator was money.

4

Motivation:
The Human Relations School

One-minute summary – The School of Scientific Management was criticised by researchers who identified the social aspect of motivation. Theorists such as Maslow, McGregor and Herzberg were all part of the Human Relations School. In this chapter we will outline:

▶ the Human Relations School
▶ the work of Elton Mayo
▶ Abraham Maslow's 'hierarchy of needs'
▶ the work of McGregor
▶ Frederic Herzberg: the two factor theory

The Human Relations School

Scientific Management means increasing production through pay, training and the best organisation and tooling (treating people as machines). In contrast, the Human Relations School argues for increasing output through treating people as human beings. Productivity is not just affected by training and monetary inducements. It is also affected by social factors as such as praise, recognition and responsibility.

The work of Elton Mayo

Mayo's name is inextricably linked with the Hawthorne Studies carried out in the Hawthorne plant of the Western Electric Company in Chicago, USA between 1927 and 1932. There are five stages to the Hawthorne Studies.

1. Lighting (1924–1927)

This experiment evaluated the effect of lighting on output. The results showed that output increased when people worked in brighter conditions; but when the lighting was turned down, output increased also. Additionally, a further group of people was observed without changing the lighting, and their output also increased.

The final conclusion was the observation itself was increasing output; workers felt more a part of the organisation; they felt important being part of an experiment.

2. The Relay Assembly Test Room (1927–1929)

This study aimed to assess the effect of single variables upon employee performance. Six female workers in the relay assembly section were segregated from the rest. Various changes in working conditions took place, for example rest pauses and lunchtimes.

Productivity increased whatever the change. The women were responding to changes in working conditions, but in the main they were responding to the fact that they were the centre of attention. This is known as the 'Hawthorne effect'. The important factors were:

(a) the feeling of belonging within the group
(b) the personal interest shown by the supervisor.

To give a current example, the British press argued in 1998/9 that Kevin Keegan would achieve more with the England football team than his predecessor. This was more to do with his style than his tactical awareness. Keegan was known as a great motivator and was able to make each and every player feel important. In contrast, Hoddle alienated players through the publication of private conversations.

3. Western Electric (1928–1930)

Some 2,000 employees of Western Electric were asked to comment on:

(a) working conditions
(b) supervision
(c) jobs.

4. Bank Wiring Observation Room (1932)

Fourteen men on bank wiring were removed to a separate observation room. Over a period of six months the group developed its own rules and behaviour. This

(a) restricted production in accordance with its own norms,
(b) short-circuited the company wage scheme,
(c) protected its own sectional interests against those of the company.

The group had developed its own unofficial organisation.

5. Employee relations (1936)

This focused on employee relations. Employees were encouraged to discuss their problems at work. This led to improvements in personal adjustment, and employee-supervisor and employee-management relations.

The official account was written by Roethlisberger and Dickson in *Management the Worker* (1939). Mayo had already put the spotlight on the studies in *The Human Problems of an Industrial Civilisation* (1933).

Abraham Maslow's 'hierarchy of needs'

Maslow produced a theory of needs based on a hierarchical model as shown below.

People tend to satisfy their needs systematically. Thus a person will satisfy his or her immediate physiological needs. Only when those needs are satisfied will that person move up to the next level of need. Until the needs are satisfied, those needs will dominate the person's behaviour.

Application of the Maslow hierarchy has consequences for the firm.

1. According to the hierarchy, 'esteem needs' will not motivate an individual until the lower needs of that individual have been satisfied. Thus it is no good giving someone an impressive job title – for example Deputy Chief Executive – if the job is insecure and the salary does not match the status.

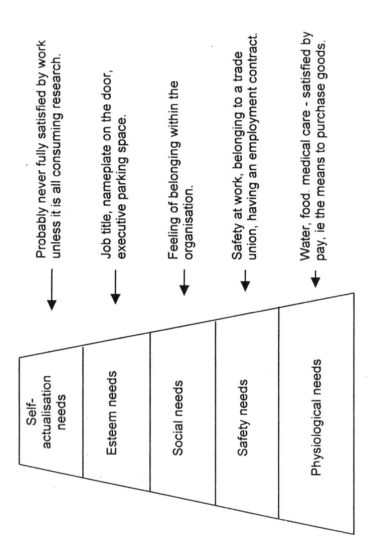

Probably never fully satisfied by work unless it is all consuming research.

Job title, nameplate on the door, executive parking space.

Feeling of belonging within the organisation.

Safety at work, belonging to a trade union, having an employment contract.

Water, food. medical care - satisfied by pay, ie the means to purchase goods.

Self-actualisation needs

Esteem needs

Social needs

Safety needs

Physiological needs

Figure 1. The Maslow triangle.

2. Unmet needs motivate. Once the physiological needs have been satisfied – probably through a wage rise – further motivation will only be possible through the satisfaction of esteem and self actualisation needs.

As with all theories, the main scope for criticism has to do with the assumptions. The hierarchy assumes that all people have the same needs and that these are then ranked in the order shown previously. This is not necessarily true; a low income person might be yearning for status symbols (not based on income) even though his lower order needs have not been met.

Not everyone has the same need for sleep, or the same need for esteem from others. Not everyone needs to be in a group and to acquire status within the group. The need for something depends on a person's perceptions, which are greatly affected by tradition, culture and lifestyle.

Frederic Herzberg: the two factor theory

Herzberg categorised factors into satisfiers (motivators) and demotivators (dissatisfiers/ hygiene/maintenance factors).

The satisfiers or motivators
These are social elements. They equate with the sense of belonging – the love needs, self-esteem and self-actualisation in Maslow's hierarchy. Motivators include:

1. responsibility/autonomy
2. recognition
3. praise
4. achievement.

Thus a worker may be motivated by a feeling of belonging to the firm, by praise and by experiencing a sense of achievement. These motivations may be more powerful than money by itself.

In his book *Management My Life*, Alex Ferguson stresses his dissatisfaction with his salary as Manager of Manchester United, especially when he discovered his salary was well below that of another manager at a less successful club side (George Graham at Arsenal). He would often ask for an increase in salary but any rise was well below his expectations. Only the continued growing success of the club kept Ferguson at the helm as offers from other Premier league teams were often made.

The dissatisfiers or demotivators

There are some factors, that if not of sufficient standard, will demotivate workers. These include:

1. pay
2. company policy
3. working conditions
4. supervisor's attitude.

These 'dissatisfiers' equate with the Maslow's lower order needs.

Douglas McGregor

McGregor identifies two assumptions about employees:

► Theory X – The employee is inherently lazy, requires coercion and control, avoids responsibility and seeks security.

► Theory Y – The employee likes work, has no need for control or coercion, seeks responsibility, and hopes to be able to exercise imagination and ingenuity.

McGregor said that theory X gave employees the opportunity to satisfy only certain needs at work (basic and security equating to Maslow's physiological and safety). An assumption that the worker was a 'theory Y' worker, would create an atmosphere allowing the higher needs of ego and self-actualisation to be satisfied.

Tutorial

Progress questions
1. State three factors that motivate people.

2. Which School of Management did Taylor represent?

3. Who or what is a 'theory X' worker?

4. What were the Hawthorne Studies about?

5. Draw a sketch of Maslow's hierarchy.

Discussion point
Are all motivational theories merely gimmicks, or do they have practical applications?

Practical assignment
Research Theory Z and discuss its current application.

Revision/study tip
The key is application. Maslow's hierarchy is all very well, but consider how it relates to business life. In all cases of motivation theory think of real life examples. This makes the theory easier to understand and to remember.

5

Motivation: Practical

One-minute summary – Different Schools of Management take differing standpoints as to the right ways to motivate workers. Often it is not possible to apply all their recommendations. For example, it may not be feasible to raise pay, and it may not be possible to promote everyone. Thus a range of other motivational techniques have evolved. Firms have successfully developed these techniques to increase production, maintain and improve staff loyalty, and engender a sense of pride in the organisation. In this chapter we will discuss:

▶ the Contingency School
▶ pay
▶ security
▶ prospects
▶ social activities
▶ style of leadership
▶ type of work
▶ trust
▶ participation

The Contingency School

The two main schools of management we have looked at so far are the Scientific School of Management and the Human Relations School. A third school, or model, is known as the Contingency School.

This states that there is no single best way of motivating the workforce – it all depends upon the particular situation. Such factors as the manager's attitude and ability, the task, and the subordinates should all be taken into account.

Thus there are a variety of factors that will affect motivation. Examples, where appropriate, are given after each factor.

Pay as a motivator

The effectiveness of pay as a motivator depends on the financial situation of the individual as well as the state of the economy. Take for example a high tax economy, in a situation where interest rates are high and a recession looms. In this case the worker may well be more worried about redundancy than the current weekly level of pay.

However, in times of economic growth, where incomes are rising the individual worker may want to be seen to keep up with contemporaries in other occupations and will require an increase in pay at least of a comparable standard. It may be possible to combine pay with training and thus offer career prospects as well as a basic wage.

The case of Craft Teak Ltd

Craft Teak Ltd is a manufacturer of high quality furniture in Trinidad, in a poorer part of that island. They recently recruited a new female worker who had just finished her GCSEs. The minimum wage in Trinidad is $7TT an hour, which equates to about 70p an hour.

The girl is to work 35 hours a week and so would normally $245TT a week. Instead, the company are putting her through training programmes which include courses in Microsoft Office, internet awareness and A-levels. This is costing the company $2300TT (about £230) and they are only paying her $175TT (£17.50) a week. The girl has agreed to work for the reduced wage owing to the training being offered. In return the company save on wage costs and after a period of time will have a well-trained employee – and still be paying less than £20 a week.

Security as a motivator

A 1999 survey by the Joseph Rowntree Foundation showed that

the greatest worry for employees was lack of job security. Even though workers' rights have been increased as a result of the Labour Government signing the European Social Contract, many workers still feel that their company is not secure as a business and may have to 'rationalise' – often a euphemism for making people redundant – to compete.

The government has to some extent reduced this fear by helping workers to become more aware of their rights. Free information about changes in employment law can be found at the web site of the publishers, CCH:

http://www.cch.co.uk

Prospects as a motivator

The prospect of promotion

The theorist Victor Vroom, in particular, dwelt on this. In his 'expectations theory', he argued that workers will work harder if they perceive that by so doing they will gain promotion.

In August 1999 the Association of Graduate Recruiters published a report, entitled *Should I Stay or Should I Go*. It focuses on the employment and retention of graduates. The report stresses that employers must satisfy the aims and aspirations of graduates, otherwise approximately 80% of them will move on. A university graduate is highly mobile in the workplace, as a result of possessing a degree. The report calculates that the national replacement of graduate employees adds up to £3m a year for those firms with the poorest records of retention.

Social activities as a motivator

An organisation may use social activities to improve the atmosphere within the working environment.

The case of Littlewoods

In mid-1999 the firm of Littlewoods was awarded the title of the country's best employer for its 'family friendly' attitude towards its 30,000 workers. The elements in this friendly attitude include:

1. career breaks
2. flexible working
3. extended paternity leave
4. paid family leave
5. play schemes and after school clubs for the children of staff
6. term-time working
7. time off for family occasions.

The results have been:

(a) A reduction in staff turnover. This has reduced employment costs such as recruitment and training.

(b) A reduction in absenteeism. This improves quality and reduces labour costs.

(c) An improvement in productivity.

(d) The publicity from this award. Where a company receives an award for the positive treatment of staff, the spin-off publicity is likely to increase orders as a happy staff equates to a high quality service, appreciated by consumers.

The award was sponsored by the campaign group Parents at Work, and by Lloyds TSB.

Style of leadership as a motivator

Leadership theorists include Rensis Likert, Fiedler, Blake and Mouton, John Adair, Tannenbaum and Schmidt, and Robert House with his 'path-goal' theory.

A leader who is strict, direct and forthright will succeed most where the task is highly structured and the worker is in need of clear guidance.

Where the leader's authority is compromised, then the poor performance by one employee may reflect on the others. This will lead to an overall demotivational effect, as all employees will be affected by the mistakes of the few.

The Exeter University study

In a study conducted in 1999 by Exeter University concluded that getting rid of an incompetent teacher can take a school up to seven years and rarely takes less than one. According to the educational inspectorate, Ofsted, up to 15,000 teachers in the UK are not up to the job.

The main areas of incompetence are said to include failure to maintain discipline, and inadequate preparation of lessons. Other factors include lack of subject knowledge, inability to deliver the curriculum, inability to communicate with parents, and failure to capture the children's interest. The failure with parents, in particular, is likely to affect the image of the school as few realise how difficult it is to dismiss members of staff.

The type of work as a motivator

The type of work itself can be an important motivator (or demotivator). This includes the level of difficulty as well as the working conditions. Many workers need to feel a sense of challenge and, after time, progress. Repetitive work that fails to stimulate may lead to boredom and mistakes.

Trust as a motivator

In addition to the job security factor mentioned earlier, workers need to feel that their employer may be trusted. This includes not only the firm's dealings with the workforce, but also in the way in it conducts its business generally.

The example of BCCI

It was claimed in a law case that the unethical and illegal way in which a banking business conducted its activities led to a stigma being attached to its employees. This stigma made it difficult for them to find other employment.

The High Court case of BCCI SA v Ali [1999] IRLR 226 was brought following the judgment of the House of Lords in Mahmud and Malik v BCCI [1997] IRLR 462. This held – for the first time – that a business conducted in a dishonest and corrupt manner could amount to a breach of the implied term of mutual trust and confidence.

The judge in the Ali case held that BCCI's conduct was sufficient to constitute a breach of the trust and confidence contract term. However, it could not be established that this breach had caused the staff involved any financial loss.

Participation as a motivator

Workers may feel the need to participate in decision-making, and also to have some degree of autonomy (see Herzberg's work). This may be achieved through:

1. employee share ownership
2. works councils
3. open-door management.

Japanese management techniques
Successful Japanese management practices include:

(a) having one canteen

(b) open-door management

(c) teamwork

(d) one uniform for all ranks up to top managers

(e) a company song. The song unites workers and helps them feel part of the organisation. (In some ways this is similar to the school assembly). Teamwork allows a degree of autonomy and shared decision-making.

Tutorial

Progress questions
1. List five practical ways in which employees may be motivated.

2. Name two Schools of Management.

3. State the name of one Human Relations theorist.

Discussion point
What factors limit the ways in which employees may be motivated?

Practical assignment
The trade union, Unison, is encouraging employees to 'blow the whistle' on employers who appear to follow dubious practices. Investigate what legal protection exists for whistle blowers in the UK.

Study/revision tip
If you have a part-time job, consider what steps your employers take to motivate you.

6

Trade Unions: Part I

One-minute summary – This is one of two chapters on trade unions. This first chapter deals with what a trade union is and how it works to further the aims of its members. In recent years membership of trade unions has declined, and unions have taken steps to boost falling numbers. It could be argued that with the increase in workers' rights there is less need for the protection that unions offer. Unions have thus evolved, and strive to be seen as partners with employers in boosting the output of the firm - at the same time ensuring that workers' rights have not been forgotten. With the growth of integration in the European Union, trade unions now look across Europe for political and economic support. In this chapter we will discuss:

▶ definition of a trade union
▶ reasons for trade union decline
▶ measures open to trade unions in furtherance of a dispute

Definition of a trade union

▶ A trade union is – 'a continuous association of wage earners that exists for the purpose of maintaining or improving the conditions of their working lives . . .' Source: Sidney & Beatrice Webb in *The History of Trade Unionism.*

Unions differ in terms of their influence, size, and representation of identifiable segments of the workforce. They also differ in structure, constitution and recruitment policies. Here are the main types of trade union:

▶ *A craft union* – one that recruits from only one – usually skilled – occupation.

▶ *An industrial union* – one that recruits only from one industry.

▶ *A general union* – one that recruits from a range of occupations and industries and is often concerned with the unskilled.

▶ *A white-collar union* – one that recruits non-manual workers with restrictions on occupation and/or industry in some cases.

Source: Heather in *Applied Economics*, page 210.

Reasons for trade union decline

Until the Blair government came into power in 1997, it seemed that trade unions were in a terminal decline. It is not just the Labour government that has helped arrest this decline, but also the policies followed by the present (1999) General Secretary of the Trade Union Congress, John Monks, who has sought to widen the membership base and change the overall union image.

Causes of decline
The main reasons for the decline of British trade unions are:

Inward investment
The increase in inward investment in particular from Japan. Japanese companies tend to prefer either single union deals or (better) no union at all. Japanese management favours greater participation and co-operation between the managers and the managed. With this partnership comes consultation and joint decision making. The product of this is job security. Increasingly UK companies, Rover for example, offer jobs for life in return for the adoption of Japanese working practices.

Legal constraints
Until the Blair government, the unions' political power had diminished. The Conservatives passed a wide range of laws in the period 1979-1997 concerning the workplace. Many of them directly curtailed the unions' powers, typically:

(a) Limitation of lawful picketing to the employers' place of work (Employment Act 1980).

(b) Outlawing of closed shops (Trade Unions Act 1990).

(c) Narrowing of the definition of a trade dispute (Employment Act 1982).

(d) Seven days' notice has to be given of any intention to strike (Trade Union Reform Act 1993).

The economic cycle
There are also the cyclical effects of high unemployment and economic recession. Richard Disney and Alan Carrith of the University of Kent tested this business cycle theory:

> 'the long-run or steady state level of union density in the British economy is negatively related to the rate of growth of real wages. For example, when real wages are growing at 1% annually, steady-state union density is 59% of employees. However, when real wages are growing at 3% annually, only 27% of employees belong to a trade union. Fluctuations in membership around the steady-state level are determined by the level and rate of change of unemployment. A rise in unemployment causes a fall in density...'

The growth in average earnings
As average earnings have risen, so the cost of going on strike rises also, as no wages would be received during the period the workers are on strike.

Increased worker protection
With the passing of legislation designed to protect the worker from discrimination, there seems to be less need to belong to a trade union. Current legislation (1999) includes:

(a) Employment Rights (Dispute Resolution) Act 1998
     Industrial tribunals renamed employment tribunals.
     Compromise agreements: independent advisor allowed to

provide advice.

ACAS can deal with redundancy disputes.

Unfair dismissal compensation affected by use of internal procedures.

(b) Working Time Regulations 1998

Restrictions on working time and rights to rest breaks and holidays.

(c) Minimum Wage Act 1998

Provides for a national minimum wage.

(d) Disability Discrimination Act 1995

Extended to employers with 15 or more employees.

(e) Unfair dismissal

Reduced qualifying period.

The growth of self-employment

People who are self-employed are hardly likely to stop work in support of a competitor!

The growth of part-time work

Often part-time workers do not belong to a trade union, because meetings may take place outside their own work hours. Disagreements with management often concern conditions, holidays and pay-rates that may have little impact on someone who only works there a few hours a week.

Measures open to trade unions in furtherance of a dispute

A union can take various actions in furtherance of a dispute:

1. All-out strike

The effectiveness of this weapon has diminished as a result of the criteria that a union must follow before actually going on strike. The outcome of the strike itself will depend on a variety of factors.

These include:

(a) stock levels

(b) demand for labour

(c) the percentage of the workforce that support the strike

(d) the financial hardship that the workforce will now suffer – and their willingness to accept this

(e) intervention by political parties

(f) public support – or otherwise – through the media

(g) degree of competition in the labour and product market

(h) the economic environment: unemployment levels; inflation; economic growth.

In mid-1999 the Trade Union Congress published its annual assessment on the state of industrial relations. Their report showed that disputes are increasingly likely to be settled before workers walk out.

In 1998 there were 166 stoppages, which is the lowest since records began (1891). The TUC polled 37 unions and found that only 464 ballots on industrial action were held in 1998 compared with 702 in 1997.

2. Picketing
This is described as 'peacefully trying to persuade workers not to go to work'.

3. Work to rule
Workers only perform those tasks specifically outlined in the original contract of employment.

4. Go-slow
Operatives make sure that tasks are performed slower than need be, paying extra special attention to every detail.

5. Overtime ban
Workers only work their contracted number of hours and refuse to work paid overtime.

Tutorial

Progress questions
1. What is a trade union?

2. Who is John Monks?

3. What factors affect the outcome of strike action?

4. What are the alternatives to strike action?

5. Why has trade union membership declined?

Discussion point
As workers' rights increase, will the role of unions further decline? If so, might not workers suddenly start losing their rights?

Practical assignment
The Employment Relations Act of 1999 increases the limit on unfair dismissal compensation. It extends maternity leave, makes trade union recognition compulsory if more than half the workforce are union members or – on a ballot – more than 40% of those eligible to vote, support it. It also bans discrimination for trade union membership. Outline the impact this Act on:

(a) workers
(b) trade unions
(c) employers
(d) the UK economy

Study/revision tip
The wider the gap between employers and employees, the greater the need for a trade union.

7

Trade Unions – Part II

One-minute summary – The previous chapter looked at what a trade union is and why membership has declined. Since the Blair government defeated the Conservatives under John Major and came to power in 1997 – and even before – trade unions have attempted to reverse the decline in their membership. They sought to appeal to a wider cross-section of members and to update their image. Employment laws are still viewed with suspicion by employers and trade unions alike, but it is clear that trade unions are once more gaining wide recognition. In this chapter we will discuss:

► why employees join a trade union
► steps taken by trade unions to increase membership
► a question about increasing union power
► trade unions in Europe

Why employees join a trade union

To avoid erosion of existing rights
Trade unions are still seen by many as a 'good thing'. Increases in workers' rights are seen as a result of trade union pressure both in the public eye and behind the scenes at Labour party conferences.

The employer is still painted as a wicked exploiter, simply waiting for trade unions to be completely extinguished before dropping workers' pay, cutting back to the bare minimum of safety regulations and deliberately discriminating against those least able to defend themselves. All this will, of course, be in the name of the need for global competitiveness and the drive for profit.

For protection
For many people, big business is once more the villain in the

world. Consider for example the issues of genetically modified food, oil slicks, and the dumping of nuclear waste. The role of the union is to protect the position of the worker.

To avoid discrimination

Discrimination in the workplace still exists, for example in the form of racism, sexism, and discrimination against disabled or older people. The publication of voluntary codes may not be enough. In July 1999 'A Code of Practice on Age Diversity in Employment' was published by the Labour Government. The code calls on employers not to use age limits when advertising for staff. To further try and erase discrimination on the grounds of age, companies are urged to ensure that interview panels are made up of mixed age employees. Promotion is to be based – it is hoped – on ability rather than age. By 2010 more than 25% of the UK workforce will be over 50. 1999 was designated the UN Year for Older People.

For incentives

Consumer incentives of various kinds are used to attract people to take up membership of a union. More trade unions offer such services as insurance, financial services, and discount cards. Unions now recognise the considerable buying power their membership represents and have been able to negotiate discounts on a wide range of facilities for their members. More than 100,000 union members carry the TUC credit card.

For job security

Security has long been identified as a major motivator for the workforce (see Maslow's needs). By having representatives to support them, employees believe that it is less likely they will be discriminated against or made redundant. In addition, if a worker feels he or she has been treated unfairly, then the union will advise what steps to take in terms of appeal against the decision.

The Employment Relations Act of 1999 gives workers the legal right to be accompanied during grievance and disciplinary procedures.

Steps taken by trade unions to increase membership

1. *Recognition deals* – Under the government's Fairness at Work proposals, workers would get automatic recognition if more than half the workers in a workplace or bargaining unit are members. In the six months to November 1998, 34 recognition deals had been signed whereby employers recognised a trade union as legitimately representing employees who were members of the union. For example, in March 1999, a group of London food workers signed a recognition deal between the specialist food group Noon and the GMB union. The recognition deals cover 63,500 workers.

2. *'New Unionism'* – In 1996 a 'New Unionism' task group was set up with a view to reinventing trade unions just as the 'New' Labour Party was also reinvented. In 1998 the New Unionism's Organising Academy was launched and attendees were taught how to spread the 'gospel of union membership'. The TUC (Trades Union Congress) believe there are 5 million potential new union recruits. They have identified the key areas of concern to the young:

   (a) low pay

   (b) respect in the workplace (young people tend to start at the bottom of any hierarchy)

   (c) insecurity in the workplace – those on short term contracts that come up for renewal every three months.

   New Unionism was further publicised by stands at Glastonbury and Reading rock festivals; the image is everything. The first intake of 36 New Unionism organisers had an average age of 26.

3. *Further change of image* – The UK government has created a fund of £5 million aimed at breaking down barriers between management and trade unions. Prime Minister Blair urged trade unions to 'Modernise and be partners in partnership'.

A question about increasing union power

Trade unions aim at consultation with worker representatives, the right to participate in key company decisions being enshrined in law. By legally involving workers in decision-making it is hoped there will be a human-face to corporate profit making.

The CBI (Confederation of British Industry) has questioned this; it sees such a partnership as a back door to an undesirable increase in union power. Unions represent 30% of the UK workforce. In Germany the representation is 29%, in France – 9%. If trade unions support changes in law that improve workers' rights, this may lead to a fall in employment. A recent survey of 800 companies was published showed that 25% of firms thought new laws would lead to fewer jobs. Only 4% saw the changes as positive (CBI *Annual Employment Trends Survey*, May 1999).

Trade unions in Europe

In July 1999, trade union leaders throughout Europe attended a conference in Helsinki. The conference marked the start of Finland's six-month Presidency of the EU. The meeting agreed to aim for a single European Trade Union, which might mean:

1. cross-border sympathy action

2. upwards convergence in salary levels

3. standardisation of working conditions

4. a 35-hour week

5. a legal right to strike

6. a 'Euro contract' which would legally link pay and conditions throughout the EU.

Pan-European strikes?

In 1997 an industrial dispute took place at Vilvorde in Belgium.

Striking car workers were joined by French and Spanish workers.

Tutorial

Progress questions

1. What is a cross-border sympathy strike?

2. What steps have been taken by trade unions to increase membership?

3. What is the current situation regarding age discrimination?

Discussion point

Is a pan-European strike involving UK workers supporting, for example, French or German workers likely, given the current state of anti-EU feeling in the UK?

Practical assignment

Go to the TUC web site and comment on one recent TUC initiative:

http://www.tuc.org.uk

Study/revision tip

Broadly, under a Labour government, trade union rights will tend to increase; under a Conservative one they will tend to be reduced.

8

Leadership

One-minute summary – What does a leader do? Obviously he leads - or does he? A 'participative' leader may lead by basing his decisions on the opinions of others. An 'authoritative' leader may not even consult others. A leader is any person who leads, but the nature and style in which they do their 'leading' will vary a good deal. Opinions differ as to the best style of leader - it seems to vary according to the workforce, the task and the external environment. In this chapter we will discuss:

▶ what is a leader?
▶ the responsibilities of a leader
▶ should a leader tell the truth to the workers?
▶ types of leader
▶ the main theories of leadership

What is a leader?

Dr Eric Williams, the second President of Trinidad & Tobago, said in his 1970 Chaguaramas Declaration that ' . . . a leader is a person who can and will give focus, direction and organisation to vaguely apprehended popular aspirations . . . '

Thus a leader must be able to articulate a direction in which the organisation ought to, and wants to, move. He ought to be able to inspire by words and example and to be able to bring his colleagues together on any issue of importance.

The Conservative politician Winston Churchill was such a leader. As prime minister during the Second World War (1939–45) he united the Britain against a common foe: Nazi Germany. When it came to peacetime there was no longer a common enemy and Churchill lost the election to Labour by a wide margin.

Machiavelli on leadership

Machiavelli was an Italian political philosopher. In his famous book *The Prince*, the wrote:

> 'As a prince must be able to act just like a beast, he should learn from the fox and the lion; because the lion does not defend himself against traps, and the fox does not defend himself against wolves. So one has to be a fox in order to recognise traps and a lion to frighten off wolves...'

Unfortunately, Machiavelli did not stop there. He went on to explain that the basic objective of a Prince (Leader) is to remain in power and hold onto it at all costs. A leader has but one objective - to hold onto power. Lying, cheating and breaking promises are all acceptable – provided the leader can hold onto his seat of power.

Has President Clinton read Machiavelli, one wonders? In her final year of office, Margaret Thatcher also seemed to put into practice Machiavelli's idea of trying to hang onto power at all costs.

The responsibilities of a leader

A leader is responsible for honouring both the legal (written) and the psychological (unwritten) contracts made between employer and employee. The employee and employer each expect somewhat different things:

What the employee expects
1. safety
2. hygienic working conditions
3. job satisfaction
4. reasonable treatment
5. respect and consideration
6. staff participation and consultation
7. job security.

What the business expects
1. duties of care

2.   obedience
3.   co-operation
4.   loyalty
5.   trust
6.   respect for the organisation's values.

Failure to honour this contract will lead to disharmony and conflict between employer and employee. The lead will be taken by the way the supervisor/manager treats his workers, the way that decisions are taken. For this leadership to be effective a leader must be able to provide direction for his workers/people. A platform must be built on which all can stand.

Workers must be proud to be connected with the firm - and the firm should be proud to be connected with the workers.

Should a leader tell the truth to the workers?

This can be a difficult matter in real life. Consider these examples:

1.   In the work environment, what will happen if the manager tells us that the company may close down within a few weeks? The key workers will look for work elsewhere. Even if the company could just have escaped closure, it will now be seriously weakened.

2.   Should customers be told that the company may fold and spare parts will be difficult to find? If we do tell them, then products will not be sold and the company will definitely fold.

Perhaps the true leader is one in whom we have faith, one we trust – and one who decides what it is in our best interests to know. We elect leaders to make decisions on our behalf. We join companies and ask for autonomy, but we still want the really tough decisions to be made by directors . . . don't we?

Types of leader

1. Charismatic
This type of leader is able to influence others purely through force

of character. This influence is rooted in personality. The characteristics of charisma can only be directed/modified by training - they cannot be taught.

▶ *Example* – 'As a manager, Alex Ferguson proved himself to be a born leader, building up total loyalty from United's fans and players. When necessary he takes care to shield his young superstars, such as David Beckham and Ryan Giggs, from the attention of the media. He has never forgotten the lesson he learnt at Aberdeen in the early eighties, that "money counts for less than finding and nurturing your own lads..."' Source: Inside front cover of *Managing My Life* by Alex Ferguson (Hodder & Stoughton).

2. Functional

The leader acquires a position of authority by the tasks he performs, which are at a high level, rather than the type of person he actually is. This type of leader will adapt his behaviour to meet a certain situation.

3. Appointed

This leader is one who has been promoted, in other words appointed to the position purely by virtue of being the next in line. The power this leader will have depends on his position in the overall hierarchy of the organisation. Should Tony Blair, prime minister of the UK become ill, then John Prescott would become Acting Prime Minister. With new-found positional power and authority, may come a different style of leadership.

4. Situational

This type of leader is simply someone who is in the right place at the right time. Arguably Margaret Thatcher was the right leader for a recession-hit country 'run by the trade unions and dictated to by the IMF'.

Through deregulation, privatisation and trade union reforms, Mrs Thatcher transformed Britain's economy. The three-pronged attack of market forces, profit incentives and growth of the private sector led, some would argue, to unparalleled economic growth from 1982–88.

Others would accuse her of dividing the country, creating a country of the 'haves' (in the south) and the 'have-nots' (in the north).

The main theories of leadership

1. Trait
This theory is based on the assumption of common characteristics among leaders. These characteristics will cause the success of the leader:

1. intelligence
2. ambition
3. astuteness
4. enterprise
5. enthusiasm
6. willingness to work
7. imagination
8. understanding of others.

2. Style theories
These theories are concerned with how leaders deal with other people, eg authoritarian v democratic leadership. According to one major theorist, Rensis Likert, there are four styles of leadership.

(b) Exploitative-authoritative:
This style is authoritarian, dictatorial, and non-participative. Communication is likely to be one way only. The style is perhaps typical of a prison governor, chief of a mental hospital or headmaster of a right-wing public school. It is interesting to note that Eton, long seen as exemplifying the very best of the British public school system, has slipped woefully down the A-level rankings (1999) and now languishes in 20th place.

(c) Benevolent-authoritative
This style is less authoritarian, less dictatorial, and more paternalistic. For example, it might be the leadership style of the headmaster of a more moderate public school.

(d) Consultative

This style involves greater democracy. The workforce is consulted and involved, and suggestions are invited. There is greater emphasis on teamwork.

(e) Participative

This style is the ultimate in democracy. It involves decentralisation, delegation, two-way communication, and worker representation on the Board of Directors.

3. Contingency theory

The main theorist here is Fiedler. His theory combines both the personality trait and the situational approach. Fiedler suggests that individuals become leader for two main reasons:

1. personality traits
2. ability to adapt to different pressures and demands.

The effectiveness of a leader's style will depend on:

(a) the power and authority of the position

(b) the task structure – how have tasks been defined, and the responsibility for their completion delegated?

(c) leader-member relations

Tutorial

Progress questions

1. What are the main characteristics of a leader?

2. What did Machiavelli say about leadership?

3. According to Likert what are the various styles of leadership?

Discussion points

1. If we accept that Mrs Thatcher came into her own during the Falklands conflict, in what type of situation do you think the following individuals would be likely to excel:

   (a) President Clinton
   (b) Prime Minister Tony Blair
   (c) Sadaam Hussein
   (d) Boris Yeltsin

   What conclusions can be drawn from your analysis?

2. 'Effective leadership must meet the demands of the age in which we live – the demands of invention, innovation, imagination, decision. It is courage not complacency that is our need today. Leadership – not salesmanship'. Comment on this statement with reference to the economic policies of the Labour government in the UK.

3. Is a manager always a leader?

4. Can you think of some charismatic leaders in the business world?

Practical assignment

The PNM party is the Opposition party of Trinidad. The Conservative party is the Opposition party in the UK. Go to their respective web sites and contrast their policies noting similarities and differences in style:

http://www.conservativeparty.org.uk/

http://www.pnm.org.tt

Study/revision tip

Leaders are not just drawn from the business and political world; they are also be identified in the sports world, the entertainment industry, health care – in fact in all areas where decisions are made. Thus it is not so much the leaders' personalities or image you have to learn about, but their behaviour.

9

The Job

One-minute summary – An easy way to remember the functions of the Human Resource Management department is to think of just one word 'job'. Their activities circle around that one term. The HRM department will write a description of, design, state the specifications of, rotate, enrich...the job. In this chapter we will discuss:

▶ job description
▶ job specification
▶ job enlargement
▶ job enrichment

Job description

A job description is a broad, general statement of details of the job. It states the total requirements of the job. This means that the applicant or job holder knows:

1. what the job is called, for example 'assistant manager'

2. what the purpose of the job is

3. what the duties and responsibilities are

4. what the activities of the job are.

The description is deliberately widely drafted in order to give the employer maximum flexibility. A narrow description limits the tasks that the job holder may be asked to do. This is particularly important if, later, the employee joins in industrial action which includes 'working to rule', in other words only carrying out the tasks detailed in the job description. The job description is often part of the employment contract.

Even when a job description is extremely vague, the employer can only make demands on the employee which are reasonable or consistent with his/her position. Thus a senior manager in a department store would not be told to go and buy ice creams for everyone on a sunny day.

Typical contents of a job description
1. title of the job
2. department/section/location
3. wages/salary band
4. duties/responsibilities
5. responsible to/for
6. specific immediate contacts (for example 'Direct supervisor')
7. signature of the head of the department
8. date.

Job specification

This is also sometimes called a 'person specification'. The job specification details the characteristics/qualifications of the ideal person for the job. The person/job specification may be based on Munro-Fraser's following five-fold grading system. This system allows interviewers to assess the applicant in five different areas:

1. impact on others
2. qualifications
3. innate abilities/aptitudes
4. motivation
5. adjustment/social skills.

Uses of a job specification
(a) selection/recruitment
(b) training
(c) promotion
(d) appraisal

(e) setting performance standards
(f) job evaluation.

Job enlargement

With job enlargement the employee carries out a wider range of tasks than before, although none of the additional tasks will be at a higher level of responsibility/difficulty. Thus this is 'more of the same thing'; a horizontal extension of an employee's present position.

Advantages to the employee

1. The employee may have been pressurising management to change the job, to change the level of responsibility. If this is the case, the change will be a motivator, even though the extra tasks are of the same level of difficulty; a change being 'as good as a rest'. As management have allowed the employee to take on more work, this could be a sign that the employer really does have the employee's interest at heart.

2. If the employee has to make more decisions, he will also have to cope with more results. This therefore provides an opportunity for him to shine. S/he will have a chance of a greater sense of achievement (see the earlier chapter about Human Relations theorists).

3. The employee may receive more credit. It is likely with the increased decision making, there will be higher status and higher pay.

   (a) This increase in pay may act as a further motivator. See the work of Taylor, Scientific Management.

   (b) Following on from the above, the average workload increases and staff become more involved. Work is less fragmented and over-delegated. The unsettling influence of a consistent stream of new recruits is temporarily halted.

Advantages to the employer

1. By increasing the number of tasks for one particular individual, slack time may be utilised.

2. These extra tasks may act as a motivator, reducing dissatisfaction and labour turnover.

3. Costs may fall as there will be less need for further recruitment and/or over-time.

Job enrichment

Job enrichment refers to giving the employee more responsibilities, making the job more interesting and giving employees the chance to extend their abilities.

According to Herzberg a job that has been 'enriched' should contain:

(a) A range of tasks at different levels of difficulty. Some of these will be relatively easy; some will be a challenge. Not all the challenges should be within the employees immediate reach. Care must be taken to make them neither too easy nor too difficult.

(b) The tasks, either singularly or combined, add up to a complete unit of work. The employee is not just doing fragmented work which can lead to alienation as he perceives himself as a small cog in an enormous, uncaring machine.

(c) Positive feedback. This will enable the employee to be aware of his performance levels. It will show him that management is interested in his work and wants him to increasingly become a key player in the organisation.

'Reaching people, helping them give that extra ounce of effort, motivating them to really believe the organisation's vision, can only happen if their managers are genuinely in touch with them. People can only be moved in this way through some form of

emotional relationship... too much management literature ana-
lyses organisations in an abstract form and fails to address the real
issues of practice that individuals need to know about. This
abstraction away from real activity and real life is one of the
outcomes of an alienation of human activity and analysis that
affects most academic analysis...' Source: *Shakespeare on Management* p83 by Paul Corrigan.

The advantages to the employer of job enrichment
The employee will be more motivated. This will lead to:

1. an increase in productivity
2. lower labour turnover
3. reduced absenteeism
4. improvements in punctuality
5. improvement in quality
6. greater compliance with requests from management.

Tutorial

Progress questions
1. What is the difference between a job description and a job
   specification?

2. What does job enrichment mean – higher pay?

3. Give an example of job enlargement

Discussion point
1. Is it always possible to carry out job enrichment?

2. What are the factors in job enlargement?

3. How may a job be enriched?

Practical assignment
1. 'Job' is included in a number of phrases. Explain the meaning of
   the following: job... analysis, description, design, enlargement,
   enrichment, evaluation, flexibility, grading, rotation and
   satisfaction.

2. Obtain the job description for someone carrying out the delivery of Business Studies to A-level students at your school. How far do the activities of your teacher extend beyond the job description?

Study/revision tip

Enlarging is less satisfying than enriching. Specification is more specific than description.

10

Recruitment and Selection

One-minute summary – Successful recruitment may be split into three stages. The first stage is identifying and codifying the requirements of the organisation. The results of this will appear in the form of a job description and a job specification. (Both of these were dealt with in chapter 9). The next two stages are recruitment and selection. Care must be taken to comply with the law as it affects recruitment, in particular the law on discrimination on the grounds of sex and/or race. This law applies equally to internal and external recruitment. Selection and appointment are the final stages of the recruitment process. Appointment includes the acceptance by both parties of the contract of employment. In this chapter, we will discuss:

▶ reasons for recruitment
▶ advantages of internal recruitment
▶ recruitment using external sources
▶ the law on discrimination when recruiting
▶ selection

Reasons for recruitment

Employers recruit for a variety of reasons.

1. The employer anticipates a rise in demand for its products or services.

2. Training is required and the employer wishes to ensure there is cover for staff.

3. Staff are expected to leave, for example those about to retire; replacements are needed.

4. Staff who have already left need to be replaced.

5. An unexpected increase/change in demand for the employer's products and services necessitates recruitment to meet demand.

The reason for recruitment is likely to have an effect on the source. If the need is urgent and the job is specialised, internal recruitment (in other words, of an existing employee currently engaged on other tasks) may be favoured. Not only may this be quicker, but the skills of the selected employee will already be known to the employer. A problem remains, though, since that employee may now have to be replaced.

There may be plenty of time before the new employee is needed, for example if three employees are needed to replace staff who have just given in three months' notice. In such a case, wider sources of recruitment may be used.

Advantages of internal recruitment

1. The employee is already known to the organisation. The organisation will have access to his personal files and be aware of his existing appraisal reports.

2. The costs of internal recruitment may be less. The overall deal to attract an outsider may include relocation costs. Recruiting from inside the organisation, unless from another branch, is unlikely to involve such costs.

3. Recruitment from internal sources may be a staff motivator. Other workers will see that promotion/transfer is possible, when internal staff are considered first. Another position may become vacant owing to the employment. (See work by theorists such as Vroom and Expectancy Theory.)

Recruitment using external sources

There are six main sources for external recruitment: advertisements, private employment agencies, job centres, universities and similar training establishments, unsolicited letters and calls, and through the internet.

Advertisements
These may produce a low response unless carefully designed and sourced. It sends information out to competitors that you may be expanding, and if a particular vacancy is repeated then this suggests unhappy staff with a high labour turnover, opening the company up to its employees being 'poached' by competitors.

Administration costs in dealing with application forms etc are incurred.

Private employment agencies
These work on commission. This will save the employer time in recruitment, as the agency will advertise and filter out unsuitable applicants. However, the wage costs may be high as they will include a substantial commission element to the agency.

Job Centres
This service is provided by the government and is free. The aim of the Job Centre is biased towards reducing unemployment, rather than (as with the private agency) finding the right person for the job. This means that unsuitable candidates may be sent along – sometimes almost against their will, since benefit may be withdrawn unless job applications are made. The time taken to interview such candidates is wasted.

Universities and other training establishments
The practice of companies visiting universities and other institutions on the look-out for top graduates and students is known as the 'milk round'. Again, although good publicity may be created, this takes time and costs money.

Unsolicited letters and calls
Large firms often receive letters from prospective applicants wishing to be considered for future positions. They enclose a curriculum vitae (CV) and hope to be contacted. The firm may write back and state that the information is 'being kept on file'. If a

post subsequently becomes vacant, this file is checked first to see if anyone is suitable; any that are will be contacted to see whether they are still available.

Through the internet

Some firms have started up on the internet offering online databases to prospective employers. People send in their CVs which may then be matched up with the needs of the employer. The employer may pay a subscription to such online services. Additional income may be generated through banner advertising.

Around ten per cent of all internet traffic relates to recruitment. The advantages of using the internet are that it is fast, cheap and efficient. Advertisements can cost as little as £6 and replies can be generated in seconds. Even if those registered on the database have to be notified by email before their details are released, the response time is still much less than by other methods.

According to a national opinion poll report in 1997, 20% of the six million people in the UK with access to the internet do not read a newspaper. Thus newspaper advertisements would miss those people.

Using the internet, potential employers can also give a lot more information about the job and location than they would be in a print advertisement.

The law on discrimination when recruiting

Advertisers must be very careful not to be guilty of sex or race discrimination.

▶ *Race discrimination* – Section 1 (1) of the Race Relations Act 1976 states 'A person discriminates against another ... if, on racial grounds, he treats the other less favourably than he treats, or would treat, another person ...'

Discrimination on racial grounds, for the purpose of the Race Relations Act, is defined as discrimination on the basis of colour, race, nationality or ethnic origin.

▶ *Sex discrimination* – The Sex Discrimination Act 1975 states that it is unlawful to treat someone less favourably on the basis of their sex: 'A person discriminates against a woman . . . if, on the grounds of her sex he treats her less favourably than he treats, or would treat, a man.' This applies equally to women and to men.

Thus, job advertisements which imply that an employer wishes to recruit someone of a particular race or gender are unlawful.

Selection

Selection of an applicant may be made after:

1. consideration of the completed application form
2. aptitude testing
3. a formal interview (individual)
4. specific psychometric tests
5. graphology (handwriting) analysis
6. short-listing and then a panel interview
7. the taking up of references.

Anti-discrimination legislation applies to selection procedures as well to the earlier stages of recruitment.

Tutorial

Progress questions
1. State one source of external recruitment.

2. What are the main advantages of recruiting internally?

Discussion point
Suppose you were interviewed for a job and the interviewer said: 'If I asked your former employee to give me just one sentence about you, what would the one sentence be?' How would you answer the question – and what would your answer reveal?

Practical assignments

1. Research the law on other forms of discrimination – disability, gender, sexual behaviour, and marital status. What exceptions are there to the Race Discrimination and Sex Discrimination Acts?

2. What kind of people is the internet best suited to recruiting? The following well-known site on the internet may give you some clues:

http://www.jobserve.com

3. Look at current recruitment advertisements and imagine the type of people the advertisers are trying to recruit.

Study/revision tip

Match your teacher's attributes to what you think the demands of the job are; this is an easy way to remember job description.

11

Promotion

One-minute summary – Not every worker wants to be promoted by his employer. Sometimes, promotion would entail a move away from home, or an unwelcome change in responsibilities. Theorists tell us that certain types of people see promotion as a motivator; others just want to stay as they are. In this chapter we will discuss:

▶ why an employee might want promotion
▶ why an employee might not want promotion
▶ the work of McGregor
▶ the work of Vroom
▶ discrimination and promotion

Why an employee might want promotion

Being promoted offers a number of advantages. These advantages – as is the theme throughout this book – may be linked to the work of motivational theorists.

Promotion may bring:

1. Higher pay (see the work of Taylor).

2. Greater responsibility (see Herzberg).

3. A change of job, or job enrichment.

4. Higher status (see Maslow).

5. The chance of even more promotion; being stuck in the same job for a long time may make other managers think an employee is not capable of more demanding work. When

applying for better jobs externally, an interviewer may wonder why the applicant has stuck at such a lowly job for so long.

6. A move away from supervisors/working colleagues which may be desired for personal reasons.

7. A change of location.

Why an employee might not want promotion

1. The employee is secure in his/her present job. The job presents no challenges that cannot be coped with. There is a low risk of losing a job that s/he can easily do well. After many years of service, forcible removal would be difficult.

2. The promotion may bring with it a change of location, hours, lifestyle and greater stress.

3. Promotion may lead the employee into having to supervise friends. For example, when a footballer is promoted to manager, he may find it difficult to exercise discipline over his ex-team mates.

4. Although promotion brings more money, the employee is now in a higher tax band and the increase is not as much as would first seem.

5. Although the basic wage is higher there is no performance-related pay, and so take-home pay actually falls.

6. There is a feeling that the promotion was biased. (The employee's new boss – his uncle – disagrees!)

The work of McGregor

The work of Douglas McGregor has been discussed before in chapter 4 which dealt with the various Schools of Management.

In his book, *The Human Side of Enterprise*, McGregor stated two sets of assumptions about workers' attitudes towards their employment. The two workers were labelled as 'theory X' and 'theory Y'.

The theory X worker

This type of employee has no ambition. S/he goes to work to earn some money, which is needed in order to live a particular lifestyle. The aim is to satisfy the 'lower order' needs such as basic physical needs and safety. The worker has no ambition and is lazy.

This type of worker responds most to rises in pay, but when enough has been earned, laziness may once again take over and output will fall. Highly structured tasks will be needed for 'theory X' and the supervisor will have to exercise tight control. According to McGregor: 'The average human being prefers to be directed, wishes to avoid responsibility, has relatively little ambition and wants security above all...'

The theory X worker would recognise the higher pay in the promotion but also the loss of a controlled environment, the greater risk and the increase in responsibility. For a lazy worker in need of constant guidance, despite the money, promotion would be opposed.

The theory Y worker

This type of worker is the opposite extreme to the theory X worker. This worker enjoys work – as long as it is not boring and repetitive. There must be scope in the work for challenge, achievement and the full use of personal abilities. Initiative is to be encouraged. Autonomy and empowerment are key motivators – this worker does not want to be controlled. The main needs to be satisfied by this work are social and self-actualising.

This is the type of worker who would want promotion as it would bring a recognition of his ability and give a sense of achievement. With promotion would come more responsibility and more autonomy.

The work of Vroom

Victor Vroom's name is linked with 'expectancy theory'. The theory can be applied to students as well as employees. For example, a student will generally try hard in his or her A-level studies if s/he thinks that:

1. only by trying hard can a high grade be obtained

2. attainment of a high grade will ensure a university place

3. university is the student's ultimate mid-term aim.

Similarly, the worker is motivated by a reward and an expectation that such an outcome is achievable if a particular course of action is followed. Thus job satisfaction will result from promotion as that is a sign of recognised achievement. Promotion – or the chance of being promoted – will motivate if promotion seems achievable and promotion itself is a sufficient reward.

Alternatively, if a firm prefers to recruit from external sources and/or reduces the layers of management, perceived promotion chances will diminish. This may cause workers to be demotivated.

The results of a study

'In a study I conducted into good practice in people management, I asked the managers concerned what they found motivated people to perform well. They all came up with answers under four headings:

(a) respect
(b) recognition
(c) responsibility
(d) recreation.'

(Source: *21st Century Manager*, by Di Kamp.)

Discrimination and promotion

As with recruitment and selection, care must be taken that the organisation does not lay itself open to charges of discrimination; all employees must be afforded equal access to opportunities for promotion.

The Campaign for Racial Equality has produced a code of practice to help avoid discrimination in the workplace. The code proposes:

1. allocating overall responsibility for the policy to a senior member of management

2. broadcasting the policy to all employees and job applicants

3. providing training and guidance for staff

4. carrying out regular reviews of existing procedures and criteria to ensure that they reflect the current state of the law

5. implementing additional analysis of the workforce according to ethnic origin and monitoring to avoid discrimination.

Tutorial

Progress questions
1. Contrast the theory X and theory Y worker.

2. Explain 'expectancy theory'.

Discussion point
In a small company the chances of promotion are fewer, and yet workers seem to be more highly motivated than those in large organisations. Why do you think this might be the case?

Practical assignment
In your own place of study, obtain the job description for a Head of Department and a teacher within the department. List the different tasks and levels of responsibilities. Then contrast the salary bands. How well do you think the salary bands reflect the differences in duties?

Study/revision tip
High achievers usually want promotion – and get it.

12

Dismissal

One-minute summary – In theory if someone is not doing a good job then the employer should be able to dismiss them. In practice, however, things are not as simple as that. Dismissal procedures have to be followed, and the employer may be called to justify the dismissal. Failure to do so may lead to claims of unfair or wrongful dismissal. In this chapter we will discuss:

▶ methods of terminating the employment relationship
▶ reasons for dismissal
▶ types of dismissal
▶ summary dismissal
▶ example of a tribunal ruling

Methods of terminating the employment relationship

The employment relationship may be terminated in a variety of ways:

1. By one side giving notice to the other.

2. By mutual agreement.

3. On the expiry of a fixed term contract.

4. On the expiry of a fixed task contract.

5. By 'frustration'. Lawyers say that a contract is 'frustrated' when circumstances prevent it being carried out. For example, an employment contract would be frustrated by unforeseen circumstances such as the death of one of the parties.

6. By breach of the employment contract.

This chapter deals with the last of these: a breach of the employment contract leading to dismissal.

Reasons for dismissal

An employee may be dismissed for any or all of the following reasons:

(a) gross misconduct
(b) gross negligence
(c) conviction of a criminal offence
(d) conduct likely to bring the employer/employee into disrepute
(e) unauthorised disclosure of confidential information.

The more serious the breach, the greater the likelihood that dismissal may be without notice. The employer must at all times be able to show that a fair procedure was followed in selecting the employee for dismissal. Failure to do this may render the employer vulnerable to a claim for unfair dismissal.

Types of dismissal

There are four types of dismissal: constructive dismissal, wrongful dismissal, unfair dismissal and fair dismissal.

Constructive dismissal

Constructive dismissal arises where the employee treats himself as having been dismissed as a result of the employer committing a serious breach of contract. This serious breach could be any of the following:

1. A cut in pay is imposed (with no change in the hours or workload).

2. The employee is demoted causing a loss of status and probably pay.

3. The employee is humiliated by his/her employer in front of other employees.

4. Serious false accusations of misconduct are made.

5. Racial/sexual harassment.

If the employee is unable to show that the employer actually committed the breach but had every intention of doing so, then the claim will still succeed. An example would be where the employee receives official advance warning of demotion.

Wrongful dismissal

Wrongful dismissal occurs where contractual terms have not been complied with by the employer.

▶ Example – The contract states that four weeks' notice is required but the employee only receives one week's notice.

The employee's rights on dismissal are two-fold: those under the contract of employment (contractual claims) and those provided by statute in the Employments Rights Act 1996.

Unfair dismissal

In order for the employee to bring a claim for unfair dismissal:

1. The employee must not fall into an 'excluded category'. In other words, he must be entitled to bring a claim.

2. The employee must have been dismissed, not resigned.

3. The employee must have completed the necessary qualifying period of employment.

4. The employer must be unable to show he had a fair reason for dismissal.

There are some dismissals that are automatically deemed to be 'unfair':

(a) discrimination – where the employee has been dismissed on grounds of disability, sex or race

(b) refusal to join a trade union

(c) membership of a trade union

(d) action that is taken by the employee on health and safety grounds

(e) the assertion by the employee of a statutory right

(f) refusal to work on Sundays.

Fair dismissal
If the employer can show one of the following then the dismissal is likely to be deemed 'fair':

1. misconduct by the employee

2. lack of qualifications or capability for the job

3. a statutory requirement which prevented the employer from continuing to employ the person

4. redundancy.

The key is that the employer must act reasonably and in an unbiased way. The employer must also have followed a fair procedure – probably one already in operation in the business.

   In dismissing an employee fairly, care must be taken that the contract of employment is still complied with.

Summary dismissal

Summary dismissal simply means that the employee is dismissed and leaves immediately; it can be categorised under the headings of wrongful, fair or unfair dismissal detailed above, depending on how it is conducted. The employer must have substantial due cause for an on-the-spot sacking such as violence or embezzlement.

Example of a tribunal ruling

In late 1999, there was the case of T&K Home Improvements Limited v Skilton. The result hinged upon a provision in the contract concerning summary dismissal. Mr Skilton was a double glazing salesman. His contract had a clause allowing his employers to dismiss him if he failed to achieve his performance target in any quarter. Three months' notice was required. However, in a separate clause (14.2) summary dismissal was allowable in the case of gross misconduct.

Clause 14.2 set out specific target figures for Mr Skilton. It went on to specify that 'if over any quarter you fail to achieve your performance target as outlined below you may be dismissed with immediate effect'. This lack of performance was thus categorised as 'gross misconduct' but there was no mention of loss of payment in lieu of notice.

A meeting between Mr Skilton and his co-directors was arranged when it became clear that the current target was not being achieved with little prospect that it would be. Mr Skilton was apparently given no choice but to resign. The tribunal was satisfied that the meeting amounted to a dismissal rather than a resignation.

Mr Skilton claimed that he was entitled to notice or pay in lieu of notice arising out of his dismissal; the employers argued that they were entitled to dismiss him summarily. The failure to meet the target was, they said, gross misconduct. The tribunal decided in the employee's favour, noting that for an employment contract to deprive the employee of the right to notice, or pay in lieu of notice or damages, there must be a clear and specific provision to that effect. The words 'dismiss with immediate effect' did not specifically exclude any right to payment and were 'at best ambiguous' with regard to the issue of pay or damages in lieu of notice.

In cases involving the 'construction' interpretation of contracts, any ambiguities are construed against the party who has drafted the contract. The EAT (Employment Appeals Tribunal) felt that the tribunal's decision that the words were ambiguous could not be challenged as being perverse.

Tutorial

Progress questions

1. State the different types of dismissal.

2. When may dismissal be 'fair'?

Discussion points

A woman fails to turn up to work because she is pregnant. Can a man be sacked for also failing to turn up to work? Since the man cannot get pregnant, is this not a case of sex discrimination, as by reason of his gender he is treated differently?

Practical assignment

Go to the following web site on the internet and note the current changes to employment law in 1999. How will these changes affect labour costs for business?

http://www.cch.co.uk

Study/revision tip

Unless a person is dismissed fairly, it must be unfair. Wrongful dismissal is breach of contractual terms.

13

Labour Turnover

One-minute summary – Labour turnover may be measured in a variety of ways. Usually it involves comparing the numbers of employees leaving with the numbers joining. A high labour turnover is bad for the firm in terms of costs and image. It is bad for the customer, too, as there will be a discontinuity in the supplier-buyer relationship. A continual fresh intake of workers does provide new ideas, but if the reason behind this fresh intake is dissatisfaction with the firm (manifest in resignations) then there will be a net loss to the business. There are various ways in which a firm may try to reduce labour turnover. In this chapter we will discuss:

▶ calculating labour turnover
▶ causes of high labour turnover
▶ the costs of high labour turnover
▶ ways of reducing labour turnover

Calculating labour turnover

Definition and formulae

'Labour turnover' refers to the rate at which employees are leaving the organisation. Thus a firm with a high labour turnover is often advertising for new workers, because a high percentage of employees are leaving.

However, it may not all be bad news as far as labour turnover is concerned. The firm may seem to be growing owing to constant recruitment advertisements; newcomers to the firm may bring fresh ideas; and their wages may be below those who have been replaced.

$$\frac{\text{Number of separations}}{\text{average number employed}} \times 100$$

In the above formula, 'separations' refers to employees who leave for any reason. The category therefore includes employees who leave for such reasons as retirement, pregnancy, death and ill-health.

$$\frac{\text{Number leaving minus unavoidable separations}}{\text{average number employed}} \times 100$$

The above formula omits people who leave for unavoidable reasons such as those given above. Care should be taken with interpretation for if the result is 50% this does not mean that there will be a 100% turnover in two years. Often, it is the same jobs that become vacant time and time again. This may be for such reasons as stress, difficulty, or low pay, as will be discussed below.

$$\frac{\text{Number with over one year's service}}{\text{total number employed one year ago}} \times 100$$

This formula is called the 'stability index'. The higher the ratio the more stable the organisation is.

Causes of high labour turnover

There may be a variety of causes of a high labour turnover. Not all of them will necessarily be within the control of management.

External causes

1. Fall in demand owing to government/Bank of England action. Examples would be a rise in income tax and/or a rise in interest rates.

2. A rise in demand, perhaps for the opposite reasons shown above. Employees thus move elsewhere to further their career or receive higher pay. (This would seem to apply in particular to professional footballers.)

3. Changes in legislation which causes the company to incur costs. The only way to reduce costs is to close down a production line/make people redundant.

Internal causes
Action by management
(a) dismissal due to workers' failure to meet production targets
(b) business relocation
(c) authoritarian leadership has led to low morale.

Action by workers
Dissatisfaction with pay and/or working conditions.

Costs of high labour turnover

If the people leaving are replaced, the firm will incur recruitment costs. These will include advertising, interviewing and selection expenses. Other costs have to be taken into account:

(a) While replacements are awaited, production falls and sales are reduced. Alternatively, other workers work overtime at an enhanced rate due to antisocial hours increasing costs.

(b) When newcomers start, they may have to be trained. This takes time and costs money. Production is still not back up to normal.

(c) Owing to constant staff changes staff, morale falls. This leads to pay claims, threats of industrial action and lack of support for management. The image of the firm suffers.

(d) If the people who leave were in direct contact with customers, the firm's image suffers. Letters written by people who subsequently leave the organisation contribute to a general feeling of instability. The rapport between sales staff and customers is lost.

Ways of reducing high labour turnover

1. Conduct exit interviews
Exit interviews are interviews conducted with employees who are leaving. The aim is to try and establish the reason(s) for

resignation. A common thread may appear – for example low pay, supervisor's attitude, working conditions. It may then be possible to make changes.

2. Reduce the amount of conflict in the organisation

'To handle conflict among your team members:

(a) Ask those who disagree to paraphrase one another's comments.
(b) Work out a compromise.
(c) Ask each member to list what the other side should do.
(d) Have the sides each write 10 questions for their opponents.
(e) Convince team members they may sometimes have to admit they are wrong.
(f) Respect the experts on the team.'

(Source: *Making Teams Succeed at Work* published by the Alexander Hamilton Institute.)

3. Consider the employees who have left

Were they right for the job in the first place? Perhaps the recruitment process needs to be altered? How efficient is the selection process? Who attends the interviews? How are employees recruited?

4. Training

Are employees leaving because they feel they are under-trained? Does the induction period thoroughly prepare employees for the tasks ahead?

5. Are the workers being motivated adequately?

Do they want a challenge, a chance to utilise their abilities? Is there enough autonomy?

'To build a staff into a team that does the best possible job for the organisation:

(a) Be friendly to staff members, but don't treat them like close personal friends.
(b) Tell them everything.

(c) If you need help, reach out into the professional community.
(d) Invest heavily in loyalty.
(e) Realise that fairness establishes your credibility.
(f) Never be too busy to laugh.'

(Source: G. Cheatham writing in *Association Source*, Florida Society of Executives.)

6. Consider financial incentives

Those that foster loyalty such as employee-share ownership schemes may be more successful than performance bonuses based on piecework.

7. Job...

Consider job... enrichment, enlargement, rotation, re-design.

Tutorial

Progress questions

1. What does 'labour turnover' mean?

2. What is the 'stability index' and how may it be improved?

3. Is a high labour turnover always a disadvantage?

Discussion point

Is a capital-intensive business likely to have a low or high labour turnover?

Practical assignment

Is labour turnover high or low at your place of study? Is it higher among office staff or academic staff? Analyse labour turnover by department area. Suggest ways in which labour turnover may be reduced. Consider whether a reduction in labour turnover is necessarily to the pupils' advantage.

Revision/study tip

Labour turnover is nothing to do with output! Labour turnover refers to the number of people joining and leaving a firm.

14

Management Fads – Part I

One-minute summary – A few years ago 'empowerment' and 're-engineering' would have been described as 'management fads'. Now, at the start of a new millennium, both terms have become accepted as part of strategic management. The key is originality – backed by finance and protection of ideas. Managers may actively encourage creative thinking to improve the organisation's competitive edge. Empowerment is not without its problems, though, especially if workers do not want to make decisions and take responsibility for them. This chapter is one of two dealing with management fads and covers two fads of the 1990s. In this chapter we will discuss:

▶ creative thinking
▶ re-engineering
▶ empowerment

Creative thinking

The management consultants, McKinsey & Co, estimate that by the year 2000, 85% of all jobs in the US and 80% of those in Europe will be knowledge-based in some way. It is knowledge that gives Coca-Cola its unique taste; and it is knowledge that enabled Intel can develop a chip faster than its competitors. Knowledge is what gives a company its competitive edge.

Knowledge can be gleaned from applied research, through the hiring of consultants – but also from the workforce. By encouraging the workforce to take responsibility, participation is improved. This 'empowerment' releases employees from the subservience that holds back creative thinking. Re-engineering involves redesigning the organisational framework of a company.

Empowerment encourages workers to think for themselves and take decisions. Both will improve efficiency. Both will add to creative new ideas.

There are several less dramatic ways to encourage creative thinking in a company.

1. Start with the selection process
Too often, job applicants are selected on the basis of their CV and referee's reports. If there is any testing, it is likely to be for aptitude and possibly numerical/comprehension tests – not for creativity.

2. Establish a creative thinking course
Typical creative thinking courses tend to be based on the works of Edward de Bono, author of many best-selling management books including *Teaching Thinking* and *Lateral Thinking for Management*.

3. Suggestion boxes
The organisation offers special prizes or rewards for original but practical suggestions. Employees are often unwilling to share ideas or knowledge. They believe that by hoarding their ideas, they alone will receive incentive awards for individual performance.

4. Establish a 'think tank'
The think tank's brief should be to come up with new ideas and follow them through to assess their practicality, before submitting them to the company.

5. Brainstorming and mind mapping
Brainstorming and mind mapping can be incorporated into all training sessions. 'Mind mapping' is a technique for representing thinking patterns. It has been developed by Tony Buzan, in particular in his book *Use your Head*.

6. Give staff the time to pursue projects of their own choice
The UK company 3M gives it staff 15% 'bootlegging time'. During this time they can try and find alternative sources of funding within the organisation. They can only do this if their own division disagrees with them over the potential of their new projects.

7. Encourage role-playing

Encourage workers to adopt the personality of someone else before they think of possible solutions to problems. For example, 'Imagine you are the Head of Department . . . ' This minimises the chance that they will be discouraged by their relatively low status in the workplace.

Creativity may be seen as the way to save the company from the ravages of recession and competition. The Japanese, for example, have developed the 'surprise and delight' feature where they work out what the customer wants before the customer does himself – and then supply it.

Re-engineering

Here are two quotations about re-engineering:

1. 'Organisations are rather like giant jellies – if you resculpt too limited a part of them they wobble back into their old form. But if you try to remould them too much at once, the whole effort becomes unmanageable and they collapse into a quivering heap. The jelly may even become rock-solid and resistant to further shaping . . . ' (Source: Richard Heygate, McKinsey & Co.)

2. 'Re-engineering is new and it has to be done.' (Source: Peter Drucker.)

Peter Drucker and re-engineering

According to Drucker there are three elements that keep an organisation alive:

1. Total quality management allied with lean management and re-engineering. This is inward looking as is described by Drucker as being 'one of the three fingers that keep an organisation alive'.

2. Innovation.

3. Exploitation of the idea.

Two types of re-engineering:
Drucker distinguishes between two types of re-engineering:

(a) the redesign of sub-processes

(b) the reconfiguring of the entire processes (which alters the strategic and competitive rules of an industry)

In simple language, 'Its essence lies in the way companies abandon their start-stop myriad of work tasks, routines and procedures and replace them with a handful of unitary processes which have been designed from scratch to operate smoothly from end-to-end starting with full customer contact and going right through to completion...' (Source: Chris Lorenz writing in the *Financial Times*, 24th May 1993.)

Thus the key is flexibility – not sticking to a rigid, out-of-date job description. There are no barriers to communication, no demarcation, no functional boundaries.

Successes in re-engineering

▶ *Example 1* – Bell Atlantic: the waiting time to be connected to a long distance carrier of your choice has fallen from three weeks to a few hours.

▶ *Example 2* – AT&T: the design to delivery cycle has fallen from 53 to 5 days.

▶ *Example 3* – IBM Credit: the time to approve and issue financing deals has fallen from a week to four hours.

▶ *Example 4* – Hallmark Cards: the time taken to get a new kind of greetings card to the market has been reduced from three years to one.

Re-engineering can go wrong...
According to the book *The Case for Core Process Redesign* by John Hagel (McKinsey & Co), there are several signs that something is going wrong with re-engineering:

1. Inadequate management attention
If management does not devote its time to it, how can we expect the workers or a department as a whole to do so? The re-engineering process needs to be overseen and supported by top management, otherwise this lack of backing may be interpreted as a lack of commitment. If management are not committed, why should anyone else be?

2. Inadequate urgency and stamina
It may take several years for the whole re-engineering process to be completed. The first six to twelve months should see a between a third and a half of the total improvement being delivered.

3. Inadequate focus
Most businesses can be analysed into five core processes. If there are too many divisions identified, it will be difficult to bring about a cross-functional improvement.

Some key buzzwords in re-engineered organisations
(a) coaching
(b) teamwork
(c) feedback
(d) customer responsiveness
(e) networked software (to share information).

Empowerment

'Empowerment' means giving employees a degree of autonomy (power to manage themselves). The employees will be free to decide what to do and how to do it. Employees will 'own' and drive change at their pace if:

1. work has a meaning. Employees must care about what they do, otherwise being able to decide on methods of carrying out tasks will not motivate.

2. workers truly believe that they do have the freedom to make decisions and it is not just tokenism. They must feel in charge of

their work and free to establish an allocation of tasks and the order in which these tasks are attempted.

3. Workers must have confidence in their own abilities. Not only must they want responsibility but they must also be able to seize the initiative and not be apprehensive about trying out something new.

4. The workers must also believe they have influence, and that senior management is listening to their views.

Problems with empowerment
We have seen in earlier chapters that not all workers welcome responsibility. The work of McGregor, in particular, polarised types of worker as 'theory X' and 'theory Y' types. An employee may enjoy freedom of action, but dislike having to account for failed decisions. The danger is that a successfully empowered employee may then rewarded with even more responsibility – but without the necessary authority to carry out the task. For example, someone made responsible for making sure wages are paid on time may lack the necessary managerial status to co-opt workers from other departments.

There are some key misconceptions about empowerment. For example:

1. It is not enough just to be in charge of certain tasks if the impact of those tasks cannot be seen. Ideally there should be a long-term improvement project to turn to once the routine tasks have been completed. Employees do not necessarily want to influence company policy; often they are more interested in participation on short-term, tactical procedures such as how work is organised.

2. Empowered workers may need instruction – not so much in how to do a task – but in understanding the impact of the task on the whole business. Empowering information includes not only knowing what to do, but knowing how things are going, where the task fits in and how it impacts on the business as a whole.

3. Empowerment must come with real authority to pass decisions, to 'sign off' orders, and to despatch unchecked requisitions.

Tutorial

Progress questions
1. Explain in your own words the meaning of 'empowerment'.

2. In what ways can a business encourage creative thinking?

3. What is meant by 're-engineering'?

Discussion point
Re-engineering and empowerment were fads of the early 1990s. Have they been replaced by newer ideas?

Practical assignment
Outline Porter's main ideas and compare them with the re-engineering concepts of Champy and Hammer.

Study/revision tip
Very few theories are fundamentally new. Most are just modifications adapted from existing schools of thought, and presented using new terminology or jargon.

15

Management Fads – Part II

One-minute summary – Recent changes in management include the recognition that it is intellectual capital that gives the competitive edge. Arguably the best strategy is to copy the strategies of others – in different fields. This way you will stay ahead of those in your own market. To fully understand the likely management fads of tomorrow we have to recognise the current management thinkers and by following their train of thought, anticipate their recommendations. In this chapter we will discuss:

▶ noisy management
▶ quiet management
▶ six management gurus

Noisy management

Re-engineering, delayering, downsizing, management of change, empowerment, globalisation – all are examples of 'noisy management'. Management books scream at us from bookshelves urging us that yet another new 'strategic approach' was upon us and yet again the world of business would be saved. Work by Henry Mintzberg, the Cleghorn Professor of Management Studies at McGill University, concludes the following about some of the noisy management words:

'Globalisation: this does not mean a global mindset ...empowerment: organisations with real empowerment do not talk about it. Those that make a lot of noise about it generally lack it. Real empowerment is a most natural state of affairs: people who know what they have to do simply get on with it, like worker bees. Change is the ultimate in managerial noise...hypercompetition, hyperturbulence; companies being turned around left and right. Leadership: the white knight rides in on his horse and fixes everything . . . '

Football clubs that have become public limited companies seem intent on finding leaders who will drive the club to success – within the constraints of shareholders imposing financial limitations. For example, Newcastle United plc appointed ex-England manager Bobby Robson (aged 66) as their new manager, convinced that he would be able to 'turn around' the club who suffered from the misfortune of not winning any of their early football matches in the 1999/2000 season.

Everything is instant. Every new fad is different. Every new concept urges you to forget all that has been taught before. Work begins at the bottom and yet success is wanted today. Success – usually – takes time. If it is immediate (disregarding external conditions) then the previous manager should have been able to spot what must have been glaring weaknesses.

Quiet Management

Henry Mintzberg draws our attention to the 'quiet' words of management as follows:

▶ *Inspiring* – Quiet managers inspire workers. They create the conditions that foster openness and release energy. When people are trusted they do not have to be empowered.

▶ *Caring* – Quiet managers care for their organisations. They prevent problems before they occur.

▶ *Infusing* – Quiet managing is about infusion – change that seeps in slowly, steadily and profoundly. Rather than having change thrust upon them in dramatic, superficial episodes, everyone takes responsibility for making sure serious change takes hold.

▶ *Initiating* – Quiet management rises up from the base of the organisation. Such management blends into the daily life of the corporation, so that people who know what is going on can pursue exciting initiatives.

Quiet management is about thoughtfulness rooted in experience. Words like wisdom, trust, dedication and judgement apply. Leadership works because it is legitimate, meaning that it is an integral part of the organisation and so has the respect of everyone there. Tomorrow is appreciated because yesterday is honoured. That makes today a pleasure.

(Source: Professor Henry Mintzberg.)

Six modern management gurus

1. Julian Birkinshaw – Stockholm School of Economics

Birkinshaw maintains that 'the essence of academic work is simplifying the complex and discovering patterns and relationships'. He is researching how network organisations identify and make best use of their core competencies. Companies are poor managers of their 'centres of excellence'. 'Companies have to identify pockets of expertise and how they can be leveraged and disseminated'.

2. Fons Trompenaars – freelance consultant and author (Holland)

Trompenaars has his own consultancy, the Centre for International Business. In 1993 he wrote *Riding the Waves of Culture* which was one of the first books to focus attention on managing cultural diversity. One of his hypotheses is 'societies which can reconcile better are better at creating wealth'.

3. Don Sull – Assistant Professor, London Business School

Don Sull has a degree, an MBA and a doctorate from Harvard. His research centres around 'active inertia', a term that describes the corporate tendency to carry on doing what they have always done when they are faced with a crisis. Sull concludes that 'Inertia is the enemy of progress. Past insights ossify into cliches, processes lapse into routines, and commitments become ties that bind companies to the same course of action. Perhaps the most vital and fulfilling element of a manager's job is to prevent inertia.'

4. David Arnold – Assistant Professor Harvard Business School

Arnold's research centres on international marketing issues and he is also the author of *The Handbook of Brand Management*. According to Arnold, 'There is a mid-life crisis in marketing. Will it go the same way as strategic planning? To some extent in big organisations it has already changed. There is now much more interfunctional marketing and marketing in business units. We are seeing the break-up of the marketing function though some central functions, such as researching new markets, are likely to remain.'

5. Chris Meyer – Ernst & Young

Meyer is an economist and Harvard MBA. In 1995 he joined Ernst & Young and headed the firm's Center for Business Innovation in Boston, Massachusetts. This is an 'R&D shop' which aims to identify the issues that will be challenging business in the future – and defining responses to them.

6. Peter Cohan

Cohan is owner of a consulting company in Marlborough, Massachusetts. His thinking is a distillation of some of the ideas that appeared in re-engineering. Cohan argues 'The source of wealth was natural resources and then manufacturing and distribution. Now it is the ability to manage smart people'.

Cohan is the author of the book *The Technology Leaders* in which he writes of a 'value triangle': 'First you have to understand customer needs, then you must identify the specific product attributes required to meet the customer needs better than your competitors. Finally you have to get the technology that delivers those attributes. Sequence is crucial. Instead of moving from steps one through to three, companies often move in the opposite direction. They fall in love with technology and lose sight of creating value for customers.'

Tutorial

Progress questions

1. Explain in your own words what is meant by 'noisy' management.

2.   Name and outline the work of one modern management guru or potential guru.

Discussion point
If the work of one theorist(s) is updated, is it necessary to know the work of the originator?

Practical assignment
Using library resources and the internet research more fully the work of the six gurus included in this chapter. Also consider the work of Kenichi Ohmae (strategy and globalisation), Ikujiro Nonaka (knowledge management) and Professor Kam-Hon Less (sinologist).

Write one paragraph that summarises the work of each of the 'gurus' and show how it directly relates to your course of study.

Study/revision tip
Early management thinkers such as Taylor (scientific management) became very popular in Japan. Asian managerial thinking is likely to be a combination of early Western thinkers and Eastern spiritualism.

16

Remuneration

One-minute summary – Wages have once more become the focus of news articles and discussion in the UK. Those at the lower end of the pay scale have become affected by the Minimum Wage Act of 1998 (effective 1 April 1999). Those at the top end of the scale have been labelled as 'fat cats' and their wages have once more become the subject of parliamentary debate. A company may pay a basic wage based on number of hours, or it may follow a wage system based on output (piece rate). In this chapter we will discuss:

► wage determination
► types of pay rate
► the minimum wage
► 'fat cats'

Wage determination

There are four factors of production, each rewarded in a different way:

1. labour – rewarded by wages
2. capital – rewarded by interest
3. land – rewarded by rent
4. enterprise – rewarded by profits.

Wage levels may be determined by demand for, and supply, of labour. If demand for the product increases, there will be an increase in demand for labour associated with that product (derived demand). If there is an increase in the supply of labour then, in theory, wages will fall. In different labour markets, there are different levels of demand and supply. It is these differences that contribute towards pay differentials.

Other factors will also affect wage levels, in particular:

1. trade unions – who may agree pay deals for their members with one particular employer.

2. local cost of living allowances – as is the case with London weighting (an extra allowance only paid to employees who work in London to take into consideration the higher wages and generally higher costs of accommodation in the capital).

3. government legislation – such as the Minimum Wages Act of 1998.

4. the pay system adopted by the employer – including non-pay items such as holidays, perks, and number of hours worked per week.

Types of pay rate

1. Time rate
An hourly rate is established for the job. This rate is then multiplied by the number of hours worked to give a total payment for the week. If the employees are able to prolong the number of hours they work, then any hours in excess of the normal working week contractually agreed, will be paid as overtime. In this way this pay system may actually act as a disincentive to work hard.

2. Piece rate
Under this system the employee is paid according to the number of items/output produced. This system is not applicable in the service industry where there is no measurable output. In order for this system to work, the output must be measurable and attributable to an individual or group of workers.

3. Measured work day
A performance level is agreed in advance with the employees; they must then achieve these performance standards to receive the (fixed) level of pay.

The Minimum Wage

The National Minimum Wage Act 1998 received Royal Assent on 31 July 1998. It provides for a single national minimum wage (NMW). It should be stressed that this is a *national* wage; no account is taken of variations by region, by occupation, or by size of company. The minimum wage covers all workers employed under a contract. This will therefore include:

1. part-time workers
2. contract workers
3. home workers.

The NMW was introduced at the rate of £3.60 per hour from April 1999. However:

(a) All 16 and 17 year olds are exempt.

(b) For 18 to 21 year olds, the initial transitional rate of £3 an hour from April 1999 will increase to £3.20 an hour in June 2000.

(c) For workers aged 22 and over, the trainee rate of £3.20 can apply for up to six months, subject to compliance with certain conditions.

The NMW applies to gross earnings and is calculated before tax, National Insurance contributions and any other deductions. The detailed rules on the operation of the NMW are contained in the National Minimum Wage Regulations 1999.

'Fat cats'

'Fat cats' is a popular term applied to directors of large companies and privatised utilities who award themselves large pay awards. Such awards are well in excess – both in percentage and absolute terms – of the pay increases offered to the workers.

The response to these awards has been a series of negative articles in the media and even a formal government investigation.

Trade unions and 'fat cats'

Trade unions in the USA have taken to publicising the salaries of 'fat cats' on the internet. The AFL-CIO, which is the American equivalent of the Trade Union Congress in the UK, has set up a web site to help its 14 million members unearth details of their bosses' pay, and tell them how to protest. Over 80,000 people access the site every day. The site allows employees to measure their total pay packages against those of the chief executives of leading US companies.

As an example, a burger-flipper earns about $13,000 (£8,000) a year at a Walt Disney theme park. He can discover on the web site that to earn the $204m that Disney chairman Michael Eisner earned last year, including new option grants, he would have to work exactly 15,710 years – and 'you can't take a vacation until AD17707'.

The site calculates that Coca-Cola chief executive Roberto Goizueta's $7.2m was enough to give 181 workers $40,000 a year. These are valuable pieces of information that may be used by trade unions in any wage negotiation claims. Management may offer 5% but if the union knows that senior management has recently awarded itself a 50% pay increase, the calls for wage restraint may fall on deaf ears. More importantly, high wage increases that may – almost coincidentally – be followed by a price rise, is bad publicity.

The government, 'fat cats' and privatised utilities

The UK government is considering giving new powers to regulators to freeze prices for customers if heads of the privatised utility companies try to give themselves big rises.

Privatised utilities face little competition and are able to make huge profits without necessarily making huge gains in efficiency. Utility directors are likely to have to reveal the links between their pay and company performance to the regulators.

In August 1999, BT chairman Sir Peter Bonfield received a 130% rise, putting his salary at £2.53m. In 1998 a survey revealed that directors of the water, gas and electricity utilities enjoyed pay rises averaging 18%.

The government, 'fat cats' and public companies

The UK government wants shareholders to have a greater influence on boardroom pay. Pay increases have to be justified by an improvement in the performance of the company. Mr Byers, President of the Board of Trade was quoted as saying

> '. . . the government has no qualms about high salaries per se, but they needed to be justified by high performance. We need to recognise that in a global economy world-class performance must be rewarded with world-class pay, but the public are aware some people are paid well for a poor performance. There needs to be a clear link between pay and performance.'

The Government proposals on pay for 'fat cats'

The Government wants shareholders to play a more active role in running companies. The belief is that shareholder activism will improve performance. To enable shareholders to have a greater role in determining boardroom pay, five proposals have been published:

1. A pay award requires a vote at the annual meeting on the remuneration committee's report.

2. Companies must publish a remuneration policy for approval by shareholders.

3. There must be an annual re-election of company directors.

4. There must be an annual election of the chairman of the remuneration committee.

5. Shareholders will allowed to put forward resolutions on pay.

The Institute of Directors and 'fat cats'

The Institute of Directors' view is that outstanding business leaders should be seen as being on a par with top entertainers and sports stars, who may earn millions. They argue that the role of business leaders in generating the wealth of the nation, in creating jobs, is not properly recognised.

Tutorial

Progress questions

1. Outline three types of remuneration systems.

2. When was the Minimum Wage Act introduced?

Discussion points

1. Which pay system – piece rate, measured day rate or time rate – is the best? If there is no one best pay system, what factors influence which method is the most suitable?

2. How far do you think pay levels should be influenced (a) by market forces, and (b) by government intervention?

Practical assignment

There is a wealth of information available at the Low Pay Commission web site on the internet:

http://www.lowpay.gov.uk

Using the information there, assess the impact of the minimum wage on:

1. low paid workers
2. employers
3. the economy.

Study/revision tip

Wages are determined by the interaction of supply and demand. Demand is derived from demand for the products. If a good or service is popular, wages are likely to rise.

17

Japanese Management

One-minute summary – Japan was originally influenced by American management thinking. They took the work of Taylor ('scientific management') and adapted it to their own factories. In recent years, Japanese management has evolved in its own way so that now UK companies look to Japan for ways to increase productivity, quality and lower labour turnover. In this chapter we will discuss:

▶ the employer/employee relationship
▶ increasing productivity
▶ company and union relationships
▶ just-in-time manufacturing
▶ 'kaizen'
▶ characteristics of Japanese practices
▶ Japanese leadership style

The employer/employee relationship

Japanese management tends to place an emphasis on individual decision-making. Decisions are decentralised with an aim towards flexible worker relationships. There is a two-way employee relationship with, again, an emphasis on employee involvement.

▶ *Example* – If a machine breaks down, then employees will either try and mend the machine or at least report the failure in order that the machine will be repaired at the first available opportunity.

Increasing productivity

A Japanese worker is always encouraged to take pride in his work.

There will even be competition between workers to try and go faster and produce at a higher quality than others.

Workers are paid in part according to their skills they have acquired. A highly skilled worker, who also works faster than the other, stands every chance of being paid more and/or being promoted. With promotion comes status (and money). Pay therefore tends to be people-based rather than job-based.

Japanese companies often follow a system of 'kanban'. This system means that for every finished product, a card is produced detailing all the different parts. Thus when there is an increase in demand for the product it will be clear exactly how many extra parts have to be ordered. Production is almost to order. Thus there are several customers in the chain of distribution – the final customer, the retailer, the wholesaler, and the manufacturer. All customers will demand low prices and high quality. All suppliers will endeavour to meet this demand.

Company and union relationships

Japanese companies prefer either no union or a single union only to represent the workers. With only one union there will be only one set of negotiations. In addition, it is unlikely that the whole union will act together over industrial action. For example, would a skilled engineer go on strike to support a cleaner?

The answer is probably 'no'. In many cases the union would be seen as an arm of management. The union would encourage individuals to work harder on the grounds that their effort will affect the success of the firm and therefore affect the pay and security of the other workers.

Just-in-time manufacturing

Japanese companies also pioneered the system of just-in-time manufacturing. This will be dealt with under three headings: social, geographical and technical.

1. Social

When a supplier is selected, the manufacturer will have checked a number of items very carefully:

(a) the financial stability of the supplier
(b) the supplier's basic housekeeping – efficiency
(c) the supplier's recruitment and training programme
(d) the reputation of the supplier.

In the car industry, suppliers are only allowed to supply one major firm. Thus if a supplier supplies Nissan there is no point in it even considering quoting for Honda, unless it is prepared to give up Nissan.

The reason for this is commercial. Every step is taken to build up a strong team. Supplier-tied research, shares sold by each company to the other, representation by each party on the other's board of directors – all encourage working together. This does give a degree of stability but also the essence of competition has gone. Realistically, there is little chance that supplies will be sourced elsewhere. However, owing to this feeling of security, both elements of the team may be willing to invest long term.

2. Geographical

New international division of labour suggests that firms will set up in countries where labour is cheap and/or there is little worker protection legislation. With the Japanese multinationals, suppliers tend to locate near their customer – and the manufacturer tends to locate near the final customer, too. This partly explains the attraction of the UK to Japanese inward investment. Other reasons include:

(a) stable political climate
(b) low interest rates
(c) trained workforce
(d) (arguably) subservient trade unions
(e) English is the spoken language
(f) pro-Europe (though this may be in doubt)
(g) government incentives.

3. Technical

Given the close links between Japanese companies and their suppliers, students may ask: why does the manufacturer not take over the supplier, in other words aim at backwards vertical integration?

The answer is one of permanence. Despite all the talk of long-term relationships, a takeover would simply be too concrete a step. In addition, owing to the trade cycle, a company may need to make stringent economies to remain competitive. What better than to ask your loyal supplier to shave his prices even more, especially after years of association?

Kaizen

Central to Japanese management practices is the concept of 'kaizen'. Kaizen means the changing of attitudes, behaviour methods, systems and procedures – it involves everyone and needs commitment. Kaizen is the process of continuous self-improvement, it encapsulates everyone: managers, staff, suppliers, distributors, and wholesalers. The kaizen philosophy assumes there is room for improvement in:

1. our working life
2. our social life
3. our home life.

Key components of kaizen

(a) customer orientation
(b) total quality control
(c) robotics
(d) quality circle
(e) suggestion schemes
(f) automation
(g) discipline in the workplace
(h) total productive maintenance
(i) kanban
(j) quality improvement
(k) just-in-time

(l)   zero defects
(m) small group activities
(n) co-operative labour management relations
(o) productivity improvement
(p) new product development.

Source: The European Japan Centre.

Characteristics of Japanese practices

Key points
1. all grades of workers have a single status – one uniform for all
2. management by walking around (MBWA)
3. tasks are allocated to groups rather than to individuals
4. company song
5. pre-work exercises
6. worker participation in decision-making
7. shared responsibility and mutual pride – workers are all responsible for the success of the company
8. job for life
9. open plan management where all workers work in the same large office
10. 'mura' – war on waste
11. 'ringeseido' – ideas are commented on by all parties.

Japanese leadership style

The Western style approach to leadership is a top-down approach. A typical objective would be to increase sales figures by a certain percentage by introducing a new product. Here the leader is highly visible; he makes decisions and keeps participation to a minimum.

Leading Japanese corporations rarely adopt such a style. Instead, the fundamental ideology is one of 'invisible leadership', which insists on encouraging ideas to rise from the bottom up. Thus when the business goes in a certain direction employees know that their ideas have been put into effect – they are therefore far more likely to support the management.

Example: Toshiba
A classic example of invisible leadership can be seen in the recent management practices of the Toshiba Corporation. The company wanted to develop products suited to the multimedia age. Their top management assembles talented personnel from within the company to form a 'Panel of Experts'. The panel is then divided into two groups.

▶ *Team 1* – sets down 9 or 10 topics ('domains') related to its members' visions for the 21st century. These should cover areas that are broadly related to the products already produced by their employers. How close this link is varies, as the team could simply be using the industry as a whole as a base for ideas.

▶ *Team 2* – takes these topics and creates product concepts and broad enterprise plans Thus team 2 works in accordance with team 1. Toshiba went further and established its ADI ('advanced intelligence, information, and integration') Project Department for developing products and technology.

In short, what drives the Japanese leadership style is the power and contribution of employees. The personnel system of Japanese corporations is extremely refined, but too fixed. The involvement of top management is required to effect change.

Tutorial

Progress questions
1. What is 'kaizen'?

2. What is meant by top-down management?

3. How does one company gain by having shares in its supplier?

Discussion point
If style of management are so different between Japanese and American/European companies, why is it that in some areas Japan is the market leader, but in other areas they lag far behind?

Practical assignment

Compare the management style of a Japanese car manufacturer in Japan to either a Japanese car manufacturer in the UK or a UK car manufacturer in the UK.

Study/revision tip

Japanese management involves all parties (suppliers, retailers, workers) as much as possible.

18

Employment and the Internet

One-minute summary – the growth of the internet has spawned a variety of new jobs in the field of web design and computer maintenance. Cyber-cafes have sprung up in many countries throughout the world. The internet has become a global community, and in that community people are now selling products/services – and looking for jobs. The internet has also meant that small businesses and consultancies have increased, specialising in the fast-expanding 'e-commerce' market. In this chapter we discuss:

▶ internet-based jobs
▶ how and where people look for jobs
▶ internet sites advertising vacancies
▶ demand for internet skills
▶ the MCI WorldCom survey

Internet-based jobs

The variety of new jobs that have been created as a result of the internet are more varied than one might imagine.

1. Web designer

The individuals who design web sites that the rest of us all view and interact with, need skills in more than just programming and graphical design. Social skills are highly sought after in this category of employee. They must not only be able to carry out the technical production of the web site, but the designer and client must meet to discuss requirements. Good communication skills are essential. Practised skills with various industry-standard software packages are also needed, which vary depending on the site content and multimedia requirements.

2. Internet software engineers

The term 'software engineer' includes those people who program the software we buy mainly as off-the-shelf packages. The job description has been around ever since computers first became widely available.

However, the software engineer specialising in internet technology requires more than systems analysis and programming skills. They have to have knowledge of internet protocols (rules), telecommunications technology, as well as security aspects: security of data and security of the computers and data connected to the internet.

3. Server maintenance

Large companies often maintain their own internet servers to enable web site users to interact with the company's database systems. Again, 'network managers' have been in existence ever since computers began to be linked together in networks for data sharing.

However, to maintain a server connected to the internet, in addition to the company network, the same additional knowledge skills are required as for an internet software engineer above.

4. Cyber-café staff

A cyber-café is a place where a number of computers are maintained with a permanent connection to the internet. Users can log on, collect and send email, surf web sites, chat to others online and take part in all the other activities associated with the internet whilst enjoying the usual facilities offered by a more normal café – snacks, refreshments, tea and coffee.

Users usually pay for the connection by the hour. Often it is possible for companies or individuals to book a whole morning or afternoon and then receive discounts. Some cyber-cafés operate a 'happy hour' in which the first hour is free or available at a low price to encourage you to spend longer online.

5. Teachers

A variety of specialist courses have recently erupted into the universities and teachers and lecturers are required to train the internet specialists of the future.

For example, the Computer Skills Centre in London offers seven and twelve week courses in 'web technologies'. There are also part time courses for learning Flash 4 (a sophisticated graphics animation software package capable of building web sites), Dreamweaver (a software package for building web sites without programming skills), and a three-day introduction to e-commerce (selling on the internet). You can find out more by visiting their web page:

http:/www.computerskillscentres.com

The University of Lincolnshire & Humberside offers no less than 13 different degree courses tailored specifically to teaching internet technologies.

6. Internet service providers

These companies – ISPs – sell internet connections to individuals and companies who either pay by way of a subscription or receive advertising and obtain the service for free. Either way every job at the ISP is there because of the internet. The people who maintain the servers, provide technical support to users with difficulties, the marketing people who arrange to advertise the companies services, in fact every discipline you will find in a FMCG (fast moving consumer good) company, will have a corresponding opposite in an ISP company. An up to date list of free ISPs is to be found at:

http://www.net4nowt.com/

How and where people look for jobs

People may look for vacancies by a variety of means:

1. Job centres
2. private agencies
3. newspaper advertisements
4. teletext advertisements

5. word of mouth
6. sites on the internet.

Although internet sites still need to be maintained it is usually the advertiser who inputs the data, by completing an online data entry form. Those looking for work merely key in their chosen job name in a search engine and a list of vacancies will come up on screen. These may then be printed out and the advertisers faxed/telephoned. Alternatively, the prospective applicant can email the advertiser direct.

Some job sites on the internet

Job search
http://www.jobsearch.co.uk
This site is a 'job bank', a searchable database of job vacancies. The database can be used both by employers and by those seeking work. Those looking for work may post their CV on the site free of charge, in the hope that an employer will also be searching the site looking for people with the stated skills and experience. An email contact address direct to the employee is provided.

JobServe
http://www.jobserve.co.uk
This site specialises in vacancies in information technology. Prospective employers supply details of their vacancies to the site. Prospective applicants register with the site, supplying keywords to describe their skills. A list of all the vacancies containing those key words are then emailed to those applicants whose key words match those of the vacancies.

Top Jobs UK
http://www.topjobs.co.uk
Top Jobs is an internet recruitment agency which has contacts in Australia, Switzerland, Poland and Ireland. It covers a broad range of vacancies, showing that companies are realising that they can use the internet for recruiting in all disciplines, not just in IT and technology.

Demand for internet skills

Demand for labour is derived from demand for the product. As demand for internet access and usage increases, so does the demand for the skills of those who can use the internet for commercial gain.

According to research in 1999, many company web sites offer little more than online corporate wallpaper. The survey, carried out by the Rainier Group, included research on the FTSE 100 companies. Of these, 26 of them failed to respond to the request for basic investor information after a wait of more than 100 days. A further 16 companies either did not have a web site, could not be contacted by email, or email contact details were difficult to find on their sites. (Source: *Internet Magazine*, September 1999.) You can view the Rainier Group web site here:

http://www.rainierco.co.uk

The MCI WorldCom survey

MCI WorldCom carried out a survey (also in 1999) and found:

1. 68% of those surveyed said the internet had reduced costs.
2. 63% said it improved the quality of customer service.
3. 75% of respondents have emailed a presentation to meeting participants.
4. 46% have met via online chat.
5. 29% of those surveyed had attended a virtual seminar.
6. 52% said that the internet improved job satisfaction and reduced stress levels.

Thus, as businesses make better use of the internet, so the demand for internet-based employment will continue to grow. If this leads to growth of the company, then jobs may be changed, but not lost.

However there is likely to be a decline in employment in the service sector as cyber-shopping increases.

Tutorial

Progress questions

1. State two areas where companies are not making full use of the internet to market their goods.

2. Write a short job description for a software engineer.

3. What are the key facilities offered by an online recruitment agency?

Discussion point

Why have many companies failed to take advantage of the internet, not just in marketing but also recruiting? What tests can be run online by a recruitment agency?

Practical assignment

Go to the following web site:

http://www.prospects.csu.man.ac.uk

Outline why this site is of particular use to students looking for work.

Study tip

The net is a new medium for buying and selling. The basic selling skills will be the same and thus the vacancies will also be the same. However, the tools by which goods are marketed have changed and so extra skills will be required.

19

Teleworking

One-minute summary – Teleworking means working away from the workplace, in practice mainly at home. Teleworking makes use of telecommunications for doing work. The numbers choosing this method of work are growing. The reasons are that both the employer and the employee benefit. There are also social advantages to society. Teleworking is not without its drawbacks, in particular insurance costs and isolation/lack of social contact. This chapter will discuss:

▶ teleworking – a definition
▶ the benefits for employers of teleworking
▶ the benefits for employees of teleworking
▶ drawbacks of teleworking

Teleworking – a definition

'The combination of telecommunications and computing tech-nologies makes it possible for work to be reorganised in time and space in a huge variety of ways. All kinds of new choices to be opened up in terms of who does what work, when, and how. Teleworking is a word which describes some of these new choices. Teleworking could take the form of working from home some or all of the time, working while on the move, working from a remotely sited office etc, but it is a mistake to regard it as any single, fixed form of employment.' Source: Ursula Huws of Analytica, an independent social and economic research company.

Benefits for employers of teleworking

1. Cost savings
The more people work away from the office, the fewer workplace facilities have to be provided. A reduction in total office occupancy means smaller premises, lower office overheads and fewer support staff. Workers are more motivated as they have greater control over their hours. This reduces labour turnover, further reducing costs.

2. Increased productivity
Less time is spent travelling to and from work. Workers thus start work in a more positive state of mind. There are fewer interruptions in the work environment, which means more time may be spent actually doing work.

3. Skills retention
There will be greater skills retention. Previously if a person moved address, perhaps because other members of the family moved, then the job was lost. Equally a mid-career break would mean a loss of job.

A teleworker can work anywhere that has a power supply and telecommunications network. Even if the teleworker changes address, the job is retained. Employees who might previously have left employment due to child care difficulties, can now continue to work part-time after maternity leave; less retraining is needed.

4. Team working
Teams may be changed, regardless of the location of the worker. Thus teams may be selected for particular tasks and then changed for other tasks.

5. Flexible staffing
The workload may change. At peak times, the worker can work longer hours without the firm having to pay overtime. The time that was previously spent travelling may now be used productively. If there is an annualised work agreement the peaks and troughs of work may be catered for.

(An annualised hours agreement is one in which a certain amount of hours are budgeted for. The worker will receive the same wage, irrespective of how many hours are worked per week, provided the total for the year matches the agreed amount.)

6. Insulation

Although the teleworker is hugely dependent on a power supply, he is unlikely to be directly affected by a transport strike, bad weather or terrorist action.

7. Customer service

If teleworkers are recruited from around the globe, the organisation may be able to offer 24-hour customer service. Using the various time zones, staff can be on call 24 hours a day without anyone having to work unsocial hours. With the growth of internet telephony this service can extend to 24-hour phone cover – without an extra premium having to be paid by the firm.

Benefits to the employee

Many benefits to the employee have already been mentioned. What benefits the firm should also benefit the employee, with a growth in profits trickling down to the employee in terms of wages. The employee makes savings in time and travelling costs, and escapes from a 9-5 routine. The other benefits include:

1. Work opportunities will not be confined by distance.

2. With the growth in leisure time the teleworker will be able to participate more in local community activities. Instead of leaving home at dawn and arriving at dusk like so many commuters, the teleworker will be able to fit in simple tasks such as meeting the children from school.

3. The work may be allocated during the teleworker's peak alertness. Some people are genetically dispositioned towards being able to work late at nights. Others are better working early in the morning. Work may now be organised round these peak times.

Benefits to society

1. If the worker is gainfully and securely employed there will be a reduction in national unemployment.

2. Teleworking will lead to reduced road traffic congestion. Think how much less traffic there is on the roads during school holidays. If the same situation was mirrored by an increase in teleworking, this would save on pollution, wear and tear on roads and the frustration and lateness caused by traffic jams.

3. Teleworking will enable those in high unemployment areas to have access to work opportunities worldwide. To be able to successfully apply for these jobs the individual must have skills in electronic networking as well as specific skills for the job in hand.

4. Workers suffering from a disability will now become employable once again. Travelling is no longer a barrier to work (and income).

Drawbacks of teleworking

1. Teleworking requires self-discipline and motivation. Some workers need the external discipline imposed by an employer. They need to have to be at a certain place by a certain time.

2. For trainees it is sometimes difficult to learn online – even with video conferencing.

3. For some, the workplace doubles up as a place for the development of social skills. Although writing skills may increase through constantly dealing with people via email and fax, the speedy interaction of a conversation is lost.

4. Teleworkers work from home; this may have an impact on their mortgage and insurance premiums. Greater security may be needed. There is also the cost of the equipment to consider, as well as ownership.

5. Although for some there is greater flexibility, many teleworkers become prisoners of their personal computers. Even with the best voicemails and answerphones, some people will still not leave messages. Therefore, frightened of missing out on an important call, the teleworker stays at home, idling away the time by surfing the internet!

6. Lack of supervision may mean that time saved by travelling may now be wasted in 'chat rooms' and surfing the internet. Some doctors have begun to report cases of 'internet addiction' alongside Repetitive Strain Injury as another side effect of this technological revolution.

7. The worker becomes totally dependent on his electrical equipment. If any item breaks down, he may become temporarily unemployable. Valuable data may be lost. He may lack the technical skills to sort out computer problems. In an office environment, there would be a greater chance of someone being available to help.

Tutorial

Progress test
1. What does 'teleworking' mean?

2. State two drawbacks of teleworking, from the point of view of the employee.

3. What benefits to society are there of a rise in teleworking?

Discussion point
Some 20,000 people work for call centres. Does growth in employment in the call centre sector mean there will be more or less work for teleworkers?

Practical assignments
1. Go to the following internet web site and outline the services this organisation offers teleworkers:

http://www.tca.org.uk/home.htm

2. What are the social impacts of the introduction of IT and flexibility of labour markets, and what are the policy implications? The following web site may be of help:

http://dialspace.dial.pipex.com/town/parade/hg54/social.htm

3. Go to the following web site:

http://www.osl-ltd.co.uk

Tuition for A-level Business Studies is offered free of charge, online. What is the possible impact of on employment in schools if more teachers were to become teleworkers?

Study/revision tip
Teleworking gives the worker freedom, but with this freedom comes responsibility.

20

Management of Change

One-minute summary – The management of change requires careful planning. Otherwise the business may end up alienating the workforce, cause a fall in productivity, lose customer orders and escalate costs! Managing a change programme requires careful planning, implementation and control. Even with these three, unless there is review, the planning may still go awry – perhaps failing to overcome resistance to the change. In this chapter we will discuss:

▶ why change is necessary
▶ planning change
▶ implementation of change

Why change is necessary

The usual declared purpose for introducing change into a business is to meet the needs of an ever-changing marketplace. The firm may wish to catch up with other companies, overtake them, or simply maintain its leadership of the field.

Changing marketplaces
The new marketplace may have changed owing to:

1. The emergence of new technologies – the growth of ecommerce and the internet has led to a huge increase in demand for web designers...and PC maintenance engineers!

2. Swings in the economic cycle. The UK may have had the lowest inflation and unemployment for many years, but companies still had to make plans for the 'millennium bug' and the possibility of the UK joining the single European currency.

3. The movement to a global economy. Some companies have already adapted to this by producing 'world goods', rationalising their brands, and standardising the format of their advertising campaigns for a much wider audience.

4. An increase in competition. Nothing makes a business compete more than the thought that competitors might eventually drive it out of existence! Just as competition offers a threat so there is an opportunity (unless all their sales are from your market) for their customers to become yours.

Planning change

Questions to ask

Key questions that management must ask of the business when planning change:

1. What is our current position in terms of competitors, market share, and previous performance against forecasts?

2. Taking an optimistic view, based on current trends, where would we ideally like to be? (For example, to increase our market share to 5%.)

3. How can we do even better than our most optimistic forecast?

What the answers could mean

The answers to the above questions may have serious implications for the business. For example:

(a) Marketing – there may be a need to reduce the number of products on offer, which may lead to...

(b) ... a reduction of the workforce, causing demotivation and confrontation with trade unions.

(c) Costs may be reduced with a reduction of the workforce, but ...

(d) suppliers may raise their prices as they will no longer be able to achieve such great economies of scale.

In order to smoothly implement these changes, all parties affected should be co-opted (or, at least consulted) in the decision-making process. Thus if products are to be reduced, suppliers should be told in advance and asked to consider ways of increasing their effectiveness in supplying components for the products that are still being manufactured.

The workforce should be warned of impending redundancies – once their representatives have had the situation explained to them – and been asked for their ideas.

Implementation of change

Implementation will be that much easier if the process of change has been agreed on by all parties. For example, it may be known that redundancies are needed, but the workforce has been asked to volunteer for redundancy long before any compulsory redundancies are introduced. If compulsory redundancies can be avoided, those leaving can do so without disharmony.

Resistance to change

The main reasons for resistance to change are:

1. Feelings of personal insecurity.

2. A feeling that the change threatens pay and job security.

3. The speed of introduction makes the workforce feel that their views and feelings have been ignored.

4. The only people who seem to have to make a sacrifice are the

workforce; the managers still have their company cars and private dining room.

The key to overcome this resistance is **involvement** and **information**.

Controlling the process of change

Change should not be introduced too fast or mistakes will be made, and the resistance of the workforce will increase. Equally if change is introduced too slowly, competitors will widen the gap between them and you even further.

The answers to the second question 'where would we ideally like to be' should have led to a series of targets being produced to measure the effectiveness and speed of change. For example, if the overall aim is to increase market share from 5% to 10%, target dates should be set out for achieving a market share of 6%, 7%, 8% and 9%. A contingency plan should be included, setting out what will be done if the targets are not being reached. A contingency plan should start off by trying to establish the reasons for the lack of success. These will be included as part of the review process.

The review process

During the review process certain questions will have been asked:

(a) At what stages of planning and implementation is there any resistance? Who is offering resistance, and what can be done about it?

(b) At what stages of the planning process were stakeholders involved? (The stakeholders are the suppliers, managers, trade unions, and employees.)

(c) Who is responsible for keeping all parties informed of the change process? Has this task been completed efficiently?

(d) Were qualitative and quantitative targets set – and kept to?

Why change fails

1. A misunderstanding of what change is – it is a journey not a destination.

2. Lack of planning and preparation.

3. No clear direction.

4. Goals are set too far in the future.

5. Change was just cosmetic – change is more than just a new poster or a management T-shirt.

6. Poor communication.

7. Previous change has been a disaster. This leads to distrust from those affected by the new proposals. The change did not work before, why should it now?

8. The business is already successful – why change it? Management seems to be putting existing stability and profits at risk.

9. Fear of failure.

10. Employee resistance.

11. Disregarding the knock-on effect on other departments/ employees.

12. Lack of training for employees.

Source: *Bullet Point* 1998.

Tutorial

Progress questions

1. Why may change be met with resistance?

2. What are the basic questions that must be asked and answered before implementing change?

3. How can an employer convince a worried workforce that change is for their benefit?

Discussion point
'We will win and you will lose. You cannot do anything because your failure is an internal disease. Your companies are based on Taylor's principles. Worse, your heads are Taylorised, too. You firmly believe that sound management means that executives are on the one side and workers on the other, on the one side men who think and on the other side men who only work.' Konosuke Matsushita, 1988 (abbreviated).

How can all the workforce be involved in change? You could develop your ideas by going to the following web site on the internet and downloading 'Change Management thinking':

http://www.vanguardconsult.co.uk/chmanth.htm

Practical assignment
Go to the following web site on the internet and skim through the virtual book on change management. Choose one of the techniques listed and explained there, and apply it to any organisation you know that is currently undergoing change:

http://www.snafu.de/~h.nauheimer/

Study/revision tip
Change will have a far better chance of success if those most affected by it are involved in the original decision-making process.

21

Communication

One-minute summary – Poor communication is blamed for failure to succeed by political parties, management and the workforce. The Conservative party blamed 'not getting their policies across' for their defeat in the 1997 election. Firms often blame marketing for a failure to sell their product. Workers may go on strike owing to a failure to communicate from management. In this chapter we will discuss:

▶ barriers to communication
▶ overcoming barriers to communication
▶ business communication
▶ government communication

Barriers to communication

Even with the development of the internet, emails, fax machines and mobile phones that can do everything except make tea, technology is widely blamed for the failure to communicate.

What technology does is to provide users with more channels. It is now possible to communicate with more people, more of the time. But the quality of communication depends on the humans involved, as well as the technology itself. Tools have to be used properly to stand any chance of working.

Human barriers to communication
1. physiological factors – disability; drunkenness/drug misuse
2. psychological factors – attention disorder
3. social factors – alienation of certain categories of workers and therefore deliberate exclusion from communication
4. cultural – cultural specific gestures
5. political – lack of power in an organisation.

Technological barriers to communication
1. technical failure – computer crashes
2. incorrect technology – emails are used instead of phone calls.
3. incorrect use – emails are sent to a person who has no computer access.

Source (adapted): *Effective Business Communication* by Richard Blundel.

Overcoming barriers to communication

1. Motivate and enthuse the workforce. Often the recipient mis-hears the message because he/she is not really interested. Personal stress may also be responsible for the recipient or the sender not communicating adequately.

2. Train staff in the use and appropriateness of all technology. When the message is urgent, try not to leave it with the temporary secretary!

3. Plan the communication network – this may take the form of a chain, a circle or a wheel.

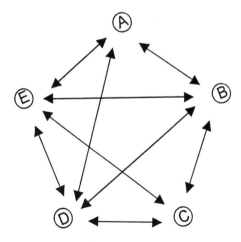

Figure 2. Three types of theoretical communication networks.

Research has established the wheel is more efficient with enhanced accuracy over the other two for simple tasks. The wheel's centralised pattern retards the group's adaptability to change. The chain is slow and the least effective of the three networks.

By identifying links of regular communication channels between members of one's own organisation, one can see where communication is absent. For example, figure 3 shows that A and C do not have regular formal contact. This kind of exercise enables management to establish whether communication is necessary, to identify whatever barrier is preventing information from flowing, and to take remedial action.

4. Develop the system of communication by reducing barriers such as status differentials. Importantly everyone must want to communicate and be aware of the importance of good communications. The chain of communication should be as short as possible to minimise mistakes. Good quality information must be easily understandable, relevant, concise, current and cost effective.

Business communication

Communicating with employees
Businesses may communicate with employees through:

1. intranet (a private internal computer network)
2. memo
3. noticeboard
4. in-house magazine
5. newsletter
6. telephone
7. company magazine
8. corporate video.

Communicating with outsiders
A business also communicates with outsiders via:

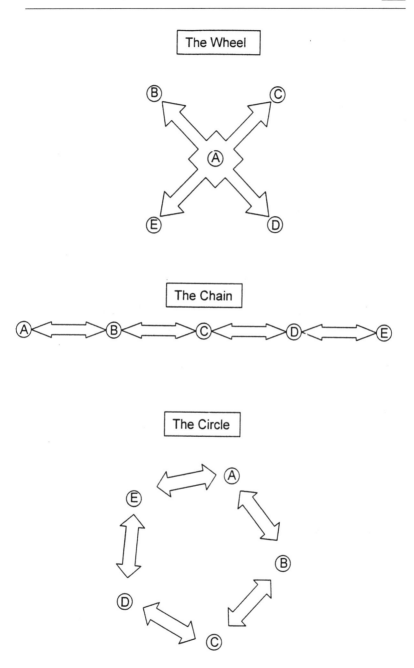

Figure 3. An organogram showing actual communication links.

1. press releases
2. formal interviews with journalists
3. the product itself
4. public relations department calling news conferences
5. corporate video
6. business television
7. email.

A business also communicates to the outside through its treatment of workers. For example, if a strike at the company lasts a long time then management may be portrayed as being inefficient, dictatorial and inflexible. Equally, a low labour turnover and vacancies advertised owing to the growth of the company will communicate success.

A company will also communicate through the issue of its company reports. Appealing reports include 'The Slug and Lettuce Group plc' and 'Groupe Chez Gerard plc'. These are both food and drink companies whose reports contain not just dry facts but glossy pictures. These may be ordered from the Wall Street Journal Europe. The web site address is:

http://www.icbinc.com/cgi-bin/wsjeu.pl

Company reports may also be ordered from the WSJE Annual reports service at Westmead House, 123 Westmead Road, Sutton, Surrey, SM1 4JH.

Government communication

Governments communicate with the electorate via:

1. press releases
2. informal briefings with journalists
3. news conferences
4. formal interviews, for example the David Frost TV show
5. pamphlets
6. manifesto.

Perhaps most importantly, governments communicate through

their behaviour and their performance. In particular the results of their efforts indicate whether they are proving to be successful/ caring and efficient. In 1998/9 the Conservatives embarked on a 'listen to the people' tour where they took views from the public about policies and priorities. By becoming more electorate-oriented they aim to be re-elected, and deliver what the populace has said it wants. The Conservatives, in opposition, say:

> 'Listening to Britain is an exercise in listening to people in all walks of life. We want to identify their aspirations and the challenges, problems and opportunities that they believe Britain will face in the future. As we have identified the problems which will face Britain in the early years of the next century, so we can develop policies, based on Conservative principles, to meet those challenges.'

Source: The Conservative Party web site: http://www.conservative-party.org.uk/

Tutorial

Progress questions
1. Give examples of the main barriers to communication.

2. Can poor communication ever be blamed on technology?

3. How may barriers to communication be overcome?

Discussion point
'The big project is a new language for thinking. Language is an encyclopaedia of ignorance. Every word came in at a relative stage of ignorance, got fixed there and forces us to look at the world in a very old-fashioned way. A new language will allow us to form much more complex concepts.' Edward de Bono.
   How does language limit effective communication?

Practical assignments
1. How can the following lead to poor communication?

(a) voice messages

(b) emails

(c) video conferences

(d) speaker phones

(e) cellular/portable phones.

2. Here is an extract from the Natural Law Party political manifesto:

'Our scientifically validated programmes will unfold the full creative genius of every student, while developing the technical skills necessary for achievement in our changing society. We will introduce study and research in consciousness, so that everyone can live a constructive life in higher states of consciousness, in perfect harmony with Natural Law – life free from mistakes and suffering.'

Go to the web site of the Natural Law Party for further information.

http://www.natural-law-party.org.uk/unifr.htm

How can research into consciousness improve communication between mankind and how will this affect/benefit a business?

3. The barriers to the growth of e-commerce and internet use in general include: legal factors, technical factors, and slow social and consumer acceptance. Discuss.

4. 'The intensive 1-day MBA will include 'Shoddipush': the deadly syndrome that white-ants most businesses'. Source: *Harvard Business Review*, 1997. What is 'shoddipush'?

Revision/study tips

Business communication is about relationships between the sender and the receiver. For communication to be effective both sides must want to send/receive, and the appropriate medium should be used.

22

Stress and Success

One-minute summary – Successful bosses seem to work the longest hours – and suffer heart attacks. In Japan approximately 20,000 people die a year through overwork ('karoshi') and yet the same country also boasts a 'Mind Gym' in Tokyo where burnt-out executives may achieve a state of deep relaxation as they recharge their short-life batteries. Is it possible to have success without stress, and if not what are the warning signs? In this chapter we will discuss:

▶ executive burn-out
▶ stress in the general work place
▶ causes of stress
▶ symptoms of stress
▶ computers and stress
▶ trade union advice on stress at work

Executive burn-out

In order to succeed in business, people are urged to work harder, increase productivity, work faster, and earn more.

Executive 'burn-out' has become a real problem in Western society. According to Professor Kakabadse, author of *The Essence of Leadership*, a burnt-out executive will:

(a) feel helpless to tackle problems they could once deal with easily

(b) will not know how to confront their predicament.

Dr Graham Lucas is a psychiatrist at London Cromwell and Priory Hospital who treats senior executives suffering from burn-out. According to Dr Lucas '... executive burn-out is the catastrophic result of prolonged stress. Anxiety and depression are minor psychiatric illnesses which predispose to, and are aggravated by, occupational stress. All these are eminently treatable provided they are recognised...'

How can burn-out be avoided?

1. Executives should have more time off.

2. Workloads need to be reorganised.

3. Overstressed people should have clear short term goals – goals that are achievable.

4. Counselling and training should be readily available; receiving such help should not be seen as a sign of weakness.

Stress in the general work place

Is stress a problem in the workplace as well as the boardroom? Stress may motivate workers. The fear of losing an order, profits, pay rises – perhaps even your job – may be a motivator. On the other hand, the fear may become so acute that the worker becomes paralysed and can no longer think clearly or work effectively.

Another response to pressure may to be to work at a frenetic pace, and hence make mistakes. When stress levels are causing problems in the workplace, efforts to control or manage the situation should focus on changing the work environment or providing affected employees with help.

Causes of stress

Physical causes of stress

1. Lack of control over workloads, over-demanding workloads or schedules.

2. Confusing instructions from management.

3. Lack of information on work role and objectives, career opportunities or job security.

4. Conflict between individuals or areas, either section rivalry or personal discrimination or harassment.

5. Poor physical working conditions, such as working conditions that are too cold/too hot or liable to excessive noise or vibration levels.

6. Concerns about exposure to hazardous chemicals or situations.

Psychological causes of stress
1. The global market and ever-increasing pace of competition has led to many so-called secure jobs becoming much less secure.

2. As time goes by workers see their jobs changing and they feel pressure to change, too – just when their own ability to change, learn and retrain is declining. Prospects of promotion are less and uncertainty starts to settle in.

3. Business contracts are increasingly issued on a short term basis; there is a greater pressure to generate profits.

Symptoms of stress

Physical symptoms of stress
1. a rise in blood pressure
2. palpitations/increased heart rate
3. aching muscles owing to involuntary tensing
4. headaches.

Psychological symptoms of stress
1. increased anxiety
2. indifference
3. passive acceptance
4. non-participation
5. depression

6. aggression
7. confusion.

Behaviourial symptoms of stress
1. increased smoking
2. increased drinking
3. irritability
4. consumption of illegal substances such as amphetamines to keep you at a state of alertness
5. obsessive concern with trivial issues
6. poor work performance.

Work group symptoms of stress
1. absenteeism
2. high or increased accident rates
3. poor or reduced work output
4. poor interpersonal relations.

Computers and stress

Are computers a major cause of stress? Computers are supposed to make our lives easier, save time and improve efficiency. A 1999 Mori survey investigated stress and computers. It found that four out of five people had seen colleagues vent their anger on computers.

One in four people under 25 admitted physically assaulting their machines, and one in six said they felt like taking their frustrations out on colleagues or office furniture. Another quarter of computer users cut short their irritations by pulling out the plug, risking damage to the computer. One third of people have to stay late or take work home as a result of computer-related problems.

Professor Robert Edelman, a psychologist who researches the causes of conflict at work, said:

'Frustration with information technology is clearly a serious issue. Technology-related anxiety is a by-product of our obsession with technology and must be taken seriously as a modern malaise. It is affecting both our work and our home lives to the extent that computer rage is now much more prevalent than the more commonly-known road rage.'

The shortcomings of computers led many workers to question whether they were more of a burden than an asset. One in eight employees had been observed bullying staff in their computer departments. (Source: BBC Online.)

Trade union advice on stress at work

The following advice is offered by the Australian Council of Trade Unions to stressed members:

▶ *Talk with your fellow employees* – See if other people at work are experiencing stress.

▶ *Call a meeting* – Ask other employees at work about calling a meeting to discuss the issues. Include your health and safety representative and your shop steward if you have them in your workplace. If there is not support for a formal meeting at this stage, you could keep the issue alive through informal discussions with other employees, and call a meeting when people feel more confident. There is no need to hold the meeting at work in the first instance.

▶ *Open a discussion* – At the meeting have an open discussion to identify the causes and possible solutions to stress in your workplace. What would make this a better place to work?

▶ *Identify the issues* – Make a list of the causes and solutions to stress in your workplace, prioritise them, and arrange a meeting to discuss them with your employer. Involve the health & safety representative and the shop steward if you have them. If your employer is unwilling to listen or to make improvements, consult your union for advice. Employers have a duty of care to provide a safe workplace.

▶ *Provisional Improvement Notice* – In some states, elected workplace health & safety representatives (HSRs) have the legal right to issue a Provisional Improvement Notice to an employer in order to remove employees from unsafe work, and which requires employers to remedy an unsafe workplace or work practices.

▶ *Refer stressed employees for help* – Employees with stress-related illness should be referred to a doctor for medical advice, and to your union's compensation officer or solicitor for legal advice.

▶ *Keep records* – You should keep a record of events in the workplace to assist in identifying the causes and possible solutions to stress. This may also be useful in assembling witness statements and evidence in the event of any legal proceedings. It is also wise to document all approaches made to the employer. If this is done, the employer will not be able to successfully argue that he/she was not aware of stress in the workplace.

Tutorial

Progress questions
1. Outline three causes of stress in the workplace.

2. State four ways in which stress may be reduced at work.

3. Stress-related illnesses account for 40 million days lost a year in absenteeism. Apart from absenteeism, how may stress cause a business to lose profits?

Discussion point
The Nuffield Orthopaedic Centre NHS Trust in Oxford recently flagged stress counselling as part of its recruitment drive for more nurses. Such frank acknowledgement that staff might need help in coping with stress is an index of how keen modern employers are to help alleviate the pressures of work. Would receiving counselling be seen as a sign of weakness or unsuitability when possible promotion is being discussed?

Practical assignment

The Health and Safety Commission have recently published a report called Managing Stress at Work. Copies of it (reference number DDE10) are available free from HSE Books, PO Box 1999, Sudbury, Suffolk CO10 6FS, telephone (01787) 881165 or fax (01787) 313995. It is also available on the internet at:

http://www.open.gov.uk/hse/condocs

Obtain a copy of the report and summarise the findings.

Study/revision tip

Managing stress is as much about job design as counselling for the person. Reducing stress may not increase productivity per hour but overall performance will improve not least owing to the reduction in absenteeism and labour turnover.

23

Personnel Effectiveness

One-minute summary – People are involved in all aspects of a business. The nuclear accident in Japan in late 1999 was due to human error (using too much uranium). The output of a company results from the combination of people and machines. The decisions taken about products and markets, about advertising campaigns and quality checks – all are taken by people. The effectiveness of people in a business depends on training, social interaction, motivation and suitability for the tasks involved. The main task for the personnel department is to make sure that not only are the right people selected for the post, but that they continue to be the right person – motivated and equipped with the required skills for the tasks. In this chapter we will discuss:

▶ labour productivity
▶ absenteeism
▶ labour turnover
▶ waste levels
▶ other non-financial ratios

Labour productivity

Why are UK products sometimes uncompetitive when compared to those from overseas? There are several possible answers. Price, design, quality, and technical efficiency are just four possibilities.

Concentrating on price, we know that price has to cover costs. Costs are made up of labour, material and overheads (variable costs) as well as fixed costs such as rent and rates. Labour costs are usually shown as u.l.c. (unit labour costs) which will be determined by output per person and wage rate per hour. The higher the output, the lower the unit labour costs. Thus UK workers may be paid more than their counterparts but if their productivity is higher, then the unit labour costs may well be lower thus giving the firm a competitive advantage.

Labour productivity thus measures output per person or per man-hour. This is the key formula:

$$\frac{\text{Output per period}}{\text{Number of employees per period}}$$

For example, if Rover employs 10,000 workers and they make 5,000 cars an hour, then the output is ½ a car per worker per hour. Output may be improved through training, organisation, bonuses and better tooling.

As productivity improves then so does labour efficiency, but if productivity grows too fast mistakes may be made. In some cases there may be a trade-off between higher productivity and safety. Certainly fatigue is one of the major problems with the payment by results pay system, where workers are paid according to the units produced. Fatigue leads to errors and quite possibly, danger.

Absenteeism

The rates of absenteeism may be affected by a variety of factors:

1. low pay demotivating the worker
2. poor working conditions
3. illness
4. attitude of the supervisor/colleagues
5. stress at work caused by discrimination/bullying.

Absenteeism is a measure of how many workers are absent from work as a percentage of the total number of workers. This is the key formula:

$$\frac{\text{number of staff absent}}{\text{total number of staff}} \times 100$$

For example, if British Rail employs 100,000 workers and on any one day 5,000 are absent, then the absenteeism rate is

$$\frac{5,000 \times 100}{100,000} = 5\%$$

If we are working out absenteeism for the whole year then we need the total possible number of days that employees could work. Thus for British Rail it could be 100,000 (workers) x 250 working days (50 weeks x 5 days a week) = 2,500,000 working days. If the total number of absences were 500,000 days then the absenteeism rate would be:

$$\frac{500,000 \times 100}{2,500,000} = 20\%$$

Ways of reducing absenteeism

1. Link pay to attendance. Thus if a person is absent one day of the week, an element of the week's bonus is lost.

2. Identify the main 'reasons' given for absenteeism and try and remove them. Thus if the main reason in any one year is health, then provide on-site medical and health facilities. This could include such things as acupuncture, reflexology and sports facilities.

3. Flexitime – this allows workers greater control over their working hours. It also means that medical appointments may be fixed at times outside core working hours and therefore in the employee's own time.

4. Improve motivation, in other words good human relations. Happy staff are less likely to be absent.

5. Involve the employees more in the process of decision taking. This confers a certain responsibility, as an employee will see that by his absence the team may break down. Teamwork may be encouraged for a variety of different levels of decisions and tasks from designing the canteen menus, to allocating work duties, to being part of an overall production team to acting as support for other teams. By reliance on peer pressure, absenteeism may be reduced.

6. Ensure that strict records of absences are kept. Then when employee appraisal takes place, question these absences. The point may be made that continued absence may mean that the employee may not be suitable for promotion as clearly the strain of work is having a negative effect on performance.

7. Engage in preventative medicine. In addition to the health facilities mentioned in item 2, management may take steps to ensure that the actual working environment is as healthy and positive as can be. This can include anything from a feng shui approach to office design, to lemon scent in the air (aids concentration and gives a sense of well being) to giving vitamin C to all workers every day. One firm of accountants in London is well known for giving vitamin C to all employees as they arrive at work. This may not actually prevent illnesses but, surprisingly, the number of absences owing to influenza have dropped to zero.

8. Establish procedures that must be followed if an employee is absent. This may include, from the employer's point of view, a telephone call home to see what is the matter with the employee then a follow-up call later to check on the state of recovery (or whether the sick employee is still at home!) From the employee's point of view, a procedure may be laid down that wages will only be paid on production of a note from the GP that clearly states what the problem is and that the employee is indeed sick.

Waste levels

The more waste is reduced the greater the reduction in costs. Waste levels represent inefficiency. The ideal for all firms would be 'zero defects'. This refers to materials but may equally apply to employees. People are recruited and then trained to do a range of tasks. If they then leave a newcomer will be recruited and trained – and costs will increase. Key formula:

$$\frac{\text{quantity of waste materials} \times 100}{\text{total production}}$$

Thus if a firm produces 400 items in one year, 20 of which are rejects, then the waste level is:

$$\frac{20}{400} \times 100 = 5\%$$

Other non-financial ratios

1. Labour stability index:

   $$\frac{\text{employees with at least one year of service}}{\text{number of employees employed one year ago}} \times 100$$

2. Percentage (%) of employees happy with the managerial style.

3. Percentage (%) of employees happy with the performance of the company.

4. Percentage (%) of requests for a transfer this year shown against percentage (%) of requests made last year.

5. Number of days lost this year through industrial action shown against the number of days lost last year.

6. Output lost through work to rule/overtime ban this year shown against output lost last year.

Tutorial

Progress questions
1. Outline two key personnel efficiency indicators.

2. Give three reasons why absenteeism may be high in a company.

3. How may employee motivation be measured?

Discussion questions
1. If personnel performance indicators are high/positive, does this mean there is less need for a trade union?

2. Days lost through industrial action may actually be hiding the discontent of the workers. How may this be the case?

3. How can waste levels in a business be reduced?

Practical assignment
Calculate the labour turnover among teachers and office staff in your place of study. What are the main reasons for the labour turnover? How could labour turnover be reduced there – and would this necessarily be a good thing?

Study/revision tip
A happy workforce is not necessarily a productive one, since contentment may be derived from not having to work too hard!

24

Working Hours

One-minute summary – British workers work the longest hours in Europe. That does not mean that they earn the most – or can buy the most with their wages. The recent implementation of the Working Time Directive means that workers may not work more than 48 hours a week (there are some exceptions to this). Trade unions object to what they call a 'watering down of the Working Time Directive' by the government. Managers say that these extra rules will lead to a rise in costs. In this chapter we will discuss:

▶ the long hours culture
▶ the health risks
▶ the Working Time Directive and its impact
▶ amendments to the Working Time Directive
▶ the business reaction to the Working Time Directive

The long hours culture

The UK has the longest working hours in Europe, according to European Labour Force Survey figures released in September 1999. UK full-time employees work an average of 44 hours compared to 39 hours in the Netherlands, 40 hours in Germany and 40.5 hours in the EU as a whole. They also receive less pay than many of their European counterparts and can buy less with their wages.

UK working hours have risen sharply over the last 15 years. In October 1998 over four million people worked more than 48 hours a week, compared with 2.7 million in 1984 (when figures were first collected.) In 1998 nearly one in five men were working on average more than 50 hours each week.

An Institute of Management/UMIST survey of 5,000 managers revealed that 77% work more than their contracted hours every

	GERMANY	FRANCE	UK	ITALY	SPAIN	IRELAND
Teacher's average hours	38	15-18	55	30	32	35
Income tax	25-53%	33%	20-40%	18-45%	Top 56%	26-46%
Beer (pint)	£0.71	£1.04	£1.59	£0.55	£0.37	£0.89
Pizza with wine (4 adults)	£25.00	£22.37	£40.00	£44.00	£25.00	£23.00
Petrol	£19.95	£27.16	£30.50	£27.00	£20.00	£27.00

Source: *The Times* - 7 December 1998.

Figure 4. Average working hours and expenditure.

week. Three out of four managers said long working hours were affecting their relationships with their partners and children.

The health risks

If people work long hours, this will leave them less time to enjoy spending the extra money they have made. For example, instead of having a leisurely meal at home they will go to a restaurant, which will cost more. The supposed income gain may therefore in fact turn into a discretionary income loss. According to a report *Paradox of Prosperity* published by the Salvation Army (1999), Britain will:

1. be increasingly prosperous in the first decade of the new millennium

2. undergo longer working hours to support elderly relatives and pay for private pensions

3. experience more stress

4. show an increase in the number of people who are self-employed

5. show an increase in the number of people living alone

6. have a greater tendency to be hooked on drugs and alcohol to counter the stress.

The report also concludes that there will be a surge in family breakdown as a result and an increasing search for spiritual meaning. Although prosperity will rise by 35%, there will be growing inequality with the top 10% of the population ten times richer than the bottom 10%.

Those families on low incomes will be further stuck in the poverty trap, as the information technology revolution will widen the skills gap. Although training is often available in local colleges, with the growth of 'teach yourself CD-roms' many skills are acquired or honed on the home computer. Even with prices dropping to under 500, a PC may still be way beyond a low-income family budget.

The Working Time Directive and its impact

The Working Time Regulations were introduced on 1 October 1998. They provide seven basic rights for UK workers:

1. three weeks' paid holiday each year, rising to four weeks in November 1999

2. a ceiling of 48 hours on the maximum average working week

3. the right to a break where the working day is longer than six hours

4. the right to a rest period of 11 hours every working day

5. the right to a rest period of 24 hours every week

6. a ceiling on night work of an average of 8 hours in every 24

7. free health assessments for night workers.

Businesses see these changes as increasing labour costs. More time off means money spent on replacements. A limitation to the working week means that extra people will have to be employed rather than extra hours worked; this will increase administration costs. Breaks during the day will simply slow down production.

Amendments to the Working Time Directive

The UK government decided to amend the Working Time Directive in several respects:

▶ *Unmeasured working time* – If a worker's working time is not measured, is not predetermined or can be determined by the worker himself, then the said worker is excluded from the provisions relating to maximum weekly working time. Under the new proposals, the regulations relating to maximum weekly working time and night work will not apply to the parts of the worker's working time which are determined by the worker himself.

▶ *Record keeping* – There will no longer be an obligation for employers to keep records of hours worked by opted-out workers. There will in future simply be an obligation to keep a record of who has signed an opt-out.

The trade union response

Responding to the announcement that the government was to amend the Working Time Regulations, TUC General Secretary, John Monks, said:

'No change to the working time regulations should be rushed through without proper consultation. There must be no weakening of protection, otherwise the government's commitment to making work family friendly will be undermined. British men work the longest hours in Europe, and we will apply two tests to the amendment. Will the proposed changes make it more or less likely that working hours in Britain gradually fall into line with those in the rest of Europe? Will bad employers find it easier to get round the clear intention of the Working Time Directive? The government needs to consider this issue fully with no snap decisions.'

The business view of the Working Hours Directive

A recent survey by the Institute of Personnel and Development (September 1999) showed three quarters of businesses believe the Working Time Regulations are a 'good thing'.

The CBI's 1999 Employment Trends Survey revealed that 70% of firms believe the Working Time Regulations, the national minimum wage and statutory trade union recognition can be implemented without any negative effects on competitiveness.

A survey of the 750 largest companies in the UK found that nearly two-thirds supported the introduction of the Working Time Directive. This does not prevent employers from abusing the Working Time Directive.

Abuses of the Working Time Directive

According to a Citizens Advice Bureau survey in 1999, some employers have been using the following measures to get round the regulations:

(a) putting workers under pressure to opt-out (sometimes to the extent that they are threatened with the sack)

(b) telling employees they are not entitled to the new rights

(c) reducing pay levels to cover the cost of holiday pay

(d) failing to give employees the choice over when they take holidays and including bank holidays as part of the three weeks' entitlement

(e) reducing other terms and conditions of employment following the introduction of the Working Time Regulations.

Tutorial

Progress questions

1. What are the main requirements of the Working Time Directive?

2. What is the reaction of business to the Directive?

Discussion point

If workers work longer hours, total production may fall. Why?

Practical assignment

Teachers' unions say that 100,000 teachers regularly work a 70-hour week. By asking a teacher you know, establish whether efficiency in the classroom would change if their extra-curricular workload was reduced.

Study/revision tip

Longer hours do not necessarily mean more production, but if the overtime is voluntary then stress is reduced. It is a matter of acclimatisation.

25

Examination Questions

One-minute summary – Examination questions on human resource management have evolved over the years. In the 1980s they were likely to be on the lines of: 'Describe the Human Relations school' or 'Outline the functions of the Personnel Department'. By the mid to late 1990s, the role of the human resources department and its integrated functions seems to have been better recognised. Questions were now more on the lines of: 'Describe how the theories developed by the human relations school have been applied in business' or 'Workers are the most important factor in a business's success – discuss.' The emphasis is now on application, not just description. In this chapter we will discuss:

▶ how essay questions have evolved
▶ how comprehension questions have evolved

How essay questions have evolved

The questions used here are drawn from the Institute of Commercial Management (ICM) Diploma in 'Business Studies' and A-level 'Management of Business'.

> 'Contrast the Scientific Management and Human Relations approach to an understanding of the behaviour of people at work.'

The above question is taken from the ICM Diploma's Behavioural Studies paper June 1994.

'Marking guidelines' are a set of rules that the Examiner marking the paper has to follow. Typical marking guidelines to answer the above question would be based on lists. In other words, a series of points would be looked for rather than specific development of those points. By the June 1999 Human Resource Management paper, the format of the questions had changed with the emphasis now on discussion:

> 'Debate the view that trade unions and/or staff associations are unnecessary to an organisation practising true human resource management'.

Note here how the emphasis is less on 'list' or 'outline' but 'debate'. The candidate is being asked, where possible, to include real· life examples as well as to define terms such as 'human resources management' – and (by implication) to distinguish 'true' management from 'just' Personnel Management.

The examiner would be looking for:

1. Definitions of key terms in the title, such as 'human resource management' and 'trade union'.

2. A development of the term 'human resource management', especially as it is applied to an organisation.

3. A clear statement of what constitutes 'true' human resource management, in other words a development of the 'personnel function' to incorporate greater development of the individual.

4. An outline of the role of a trade union – in particular their role in 'protecting/ representing' workers from management.

5. A further development of the human resource management function to show how greater participation in decision making, greater consultation and involvement of workers would mean that decisions were partly taken by workers and so no 'protection' is needed.

Essay titles for the 'Management of Business' paper have also changed. In 1986 candidates were asked:

Why is training and development important to a company? (*4 marks*)

Describe two types of training commonly used by companies for their employees. (*4 marks*)

Discuss Maslow's 'Hierarchy of Needs'. (*12 marks*)

Clearly this question is asking candidates to explain, describe and discuss. The discussion element is the major part of the question, and yet no guidelines are given as to the line the discussion should take. Candidates would not have known whether the discussion should include criticisms, application, details of the research leading to the conclusions or just a diagram plus narrative.

By June 1996, question-setters had moved away from a structured question and seemed to prefer an application of theories learned:

> 'Discuss the extent to which you consider that one of the theories of motivation which you have studied is relevant to the management of a chain of international hotels'.

Here the candidate is being asked not just to outline a theory of motivation but to evaluate its relevance to a practical situation.

This move away from structured questions towards 'discussion' type questions seems to have been followed by all the A-level boards.

How comprehension questions have evolved

To illustrate the evolution we will use a fictitious newspaper article based on real events in the late 1980s (Figure 5).

Question comparison – typical 1980s style questions

1. Explain how banks will have more profits to pay wage increases when interest rates are high. (*4 marks*)

2. How does industry lose out when interest rates are high? (*4 marks*)

HIGH INTEREST RATES, HIGH POUND

High interest rates seem to be the order of the day. While banks make more profits, industry loses out. The response of firms such as Hoover, have been to cut costs wherever they can. We all know where these costs lie: workers. If there is less demand from consumers then there is less need to employ so many workers and less need to have so many staff in shops. Trade Unions are angry but the more enlightened among them will realise that a strike would be counter-productive.

The pound is also high in part because of the UK's self-sufficiency in oil and the consequent petro-currency status of the pound. [Author's note: The UK had been self-sufficient since 1980 and by 1985 the trade surplus in oil had peaked at £8.1bn.]

Figure 5. Interest rates and the pound.

3. What is a trade surplus? (*2 marks*)

4. How might a trade surplus affect the exchange rate? (*6 marks*)

5. How does a combination of high interest rates and a high pound lead to Hoover making people redundant? (*9 marks*)

Question comparison – typical 1990s style questions

1. Define the terms:

   (a) interest rates
   (b) exchange rates
   (c) petro-currency (*6 marks*)

2. Outline one other possible response Hoover could have made apart from making workers redundant? (*4 marks*)

3. Explain how a strike would be 'counter-productive'? (*5 marks*)

4. Evaluate what options are available to Trade Unions (within the current legislation) when faced with the redundancies of their workers. (*10 marks*)

Note: these questions are not supposed to illustrate the policy of any particular examination board but merely to show how questions have typically evolved.

How the 1990s questions differ from the 1980s

(a) Knowledge of factors outside the question is required (current legislation).

(b) A discussion and evaluation of the options available is required. This means that the candidate has to assess, and then make a judgement. The candidate must therefore assimilate information and then use his own knowledge to reach a decision. The 1980s questions tended to be more descriptive with a greater emphasis on learning lists of key points without necessarily any evaluative skills.

Tutorial

Progress questions

1. Questions set in the late 1990s tended to ask for evaluative skills. In what ways do these skills differ from those required in the 1980s?

2. In what way do the 1990s questions place a greater reliance on current knowledge?

Discussion point

In the 1980s students were encouraged to learn lists of 'key facts'. In what ways has the learning process changed? Is this a positive change?

Practical assignment

1. Look at old examination papers and change the words 'list', 'describe' and 'outline' with 'applied', 'evaluate' and 'discuss'. See what a difference it makes! Get the more recent examination papers and make sure you are familiar with the format your examination will take.

2. What does the examiner mean by the following terms:
   (a) analyse
   (b) analysis
   (c) assess
   (d) debate
   (e) define
   (f) describe
   (g) discuss
   (h) distinguish
   (i) evaluate
   (j) examine
   (k) explain
   (l) illustrate
   (m) outline

Revision/study tip

Prepare for your examination by devoting time to assimilating and applying textbook knowledge to current events. For example, when studying motivation theory, think how it applies today – not at the time the theories were first developed. Although the questions may have been set a year or two ago, they are being marked in the present. This is not a History examination! However, when the question says '...from the passage' then outside material is not required.

Glossary

absenteeism A measure of how many workers are absent from work as a percentage of the total number of workers.

autonomy Self-management, being responsible for oneself.

brainstorming The free exchange of ideas however crazy they may seem.

capital The money used in a firm.

Classical School of Management This laid down fourteen principles of management, including stability of tenure, planning, centralisation and esprit de corps. The main theorist was Fayol.

contingency plan An alternative plan setting out what will be done if the main plan fails.

Contingency School of Management The school of thought that accepts that there is no one best way of management.

co-opted Brought in, instructed to join. For example, co-opted onto a committee.

craft union A union that recruits from only one - usually skilled - occupation.

creative thinking The thought process that may lead to an innovative solution. Creative thinking thrives in flexible organisation and is stifled by rigid, bureaucratic structures.

discrimination Unfair selection or treatment for example on the grounds of race, gender, sexuality or age.

e-commerce Short for 'electronic commerce', business conducted over the internet.

email Electronic mail. Messages and files sent and received using the internet.

empowerment Giving someone more control over what they do and how they do it.

'fat cats' Slang phrase for top managers, especially in the public utilities, who receive large pay awards far in excess of those of their work forces.

FMCG Fast-moving consumer goods.

general union A union that recruits from a range of occupations and industries, and is often concerned with the unskilled.

graphology Handwriting analysis.

gross earnings Pay calculated before the deduction of tax, National Insurance contributions, pension contributions and any other deductions.

gross misconduct Misconduct so serious (eg involving violence or dishonesty) that it would justify the instant dismissal of the employee concerned.

hierarchy A rigid organisational framework based on different levels.

human resources management This concerns the human side of the management of enterprises and employees' relations with firms.

implementation Putting into effect, for example implementing a plan of action.

industrial union A union that recruits only from one industry.

industrial tribunal A place of adjudication on disputes between employees and employers, where the proceedings are less formal than in a court of law.

innovation The introduction of new products or business processes.

job description A broad, general statement of details of the job. It states the total requirements of the job.

job specification A document which details the characteristics/ qualifications of the ideal person for a particular job.

just-in-time The process of stock control that minimises stock and relies on new deliveries arriving just in time.

kaizen A Japanese word for the process of continuous self-improvement. It encapsulates everyone: managers, staff, suppliers, distributors, and wholesalers. The kaizen philosophy assumes there is room for improvement in all aspects of life both in the workplace and outside it.

kanban A Japanese system whereby the kanban order card triggers fresh production of components needed for other components.

labour turnover A measure of the rate of change of a firm's workforce.

manager Someone within an organisation who is responsible for leading, guiding and controlling other employees.

'milk round' The practice of companies visiting universities and other institutions on the lookout to recruit top graduates and students.

National Insurance A form of payroll tax to which employer and employee each contribute a percentage on a sliding scale.

OTE On-target earnings: the money which an employee will earn if he meets certain performance targets.

overtime Time worked in excess of the normal hours of work specified in a contract of employment.

pay differential The difference in level of pay between two or more groups of employees.

performance indicator Any suitable method of measuring the productivity or efficiency of a business or its employees.

personnel management The passive management of recruiting, training and the discipline of staff. (Human Resource Management is personnel management with much greater involvement.)

piece rate A wage system based on output.

productivity A measure of how efficiently a firm and its workers produce their products or services.

psychometric tests Tests designed to measure personality, attitudes and likely behaviour.

re-engineering The re-design or reconfiguring of business processes.

ringeseido A Japanese business practice in which ideas are commented on by all parties.

Scientific School of Management The father of Scientific Management, F. W. Taylor, saw the main ways of increasing productivity as tooling, training, pay and better organisation. According to the Scientific School, business decisions should be made on the basis of thorough, scientific research. The Human aspect of management is omitted.

server Any computer that provides ('serves') information for people, for example a web server, news server or email server.

teleworking Working away from the workplace, usually at home, by making use of telecommunications.

top down management A style of management in which all the main decisions are taken by the top managers, and handed down to the workforce to carry out.

unfair dismissal The dismissal of an employee for a reason that is not conducted in a fair manner. Fair dismissal includes dismissing someone for reasons such as gross misconduct, redundancy and competence.

vertical integration The merger between a supplier and its distributor, a retailer and the manufacturer or any two (or more) firms at different stages of production within the same market. Example: a brewery which owns one or more pubs.

weighting An extra allowance paid to employees whose employment involves extra expenses. For example 'London weighting' may be paid to employees working in London where accommodation costs are generally higher.

white-collar union A union that recruits non-manual workers with restrictions on occupation and/or industry in some cases.

Working Time Directive A ruling from the European Commission that covers the rights of workers.

wrongful dismissal Where a person has not been dismissed in accordance with his contractual terms. Therefore he may take his employer to court for breach of contract. An example would be giving two weeks notice instead of the agreed four weeks.

Web Sites for
Human Resource Management

One-minute summary – The internet, or world wide web, is an amazingly useful resource, giving the student nearly free and almost immediate information on any topic. Ignore this vast and valuable store of materials at your peril! The following list of web sites may be helpful for your further readings on Business Studies and Human Resource Management.

Please note that neither the author nor the publisher is responsible for content or opinions expressed on the sites listed, which are simply intended to offer starting points for students of Business Management. Also, please remember that the internet is a fast-evolving environment, and links may come and go.

If you have some favourite Human Resources sites you would like to see mentioned in future editions of this book, please write to Chris Sivewright, c/o Studymates (address on back cover), or email him at:

chrissivewright@studymates.co.uk

You will find a free selection of useful and readymade student links for Business Management and many other subjects at the Studymates web site:

http://www.studymates.co.uk

Happy surfing!

Academic courses

Universities & Colleges Admissions Service (UCAS)
http://www.ucas.ac.uk/
If you are looking for a university-based Human Resource

Management/Personnel Management course in the UK, this is definitely the place to start. The UCAS searchable web site contains links to thousands of higher education courses of every description.

Professional associations

Confederation of British Industry (CBI)
http://www.cbi.org.uk
The CBI is widely acknowledged as the voice of British business. Its views on all business issues are sought by government at the highest levels. It represents companies from every sector from manufacturing to retailing, agriculture to construction, hi-tech to finance, and transport to consultancy.

Institution of Occupational Safety and Health
http://www.iosh.co.uk/
Its members include individuals with a professional involvement in occupational safety and health.

Institute of Personnel & Development
http://www.ipd.co.uk
The IPD has almost 100,000 members and is the professional institute for those involved in the management and development of people.

Online HRM resources

Department for Education and Employment
http://www.dfee.gov.uk/

Employment Service
http://www.employmentservice.gov.uk/

Health and Safety Executive
http://www.open.gov.uk/hse/hsehome.htm

Leadership Trust

http://www.leadership.co.uk/

The Trust is the largest provider of open leadership development programmes in the UK. Every year more than 1,000 delegates from all over the world attend its programmes. They come from all walks of life, from the commercial to the public sector, from the armed forces to the teaching profession.

National Training Organisation

http://www.nto-nc.org

The NTC is a representative body for UK education and training organisations, providing a link between them, the government and the European Union.

Personnel & Development Network

http://www.pdn.co.uk/indexn.htm

The PDN site acts as an electronic hub from which you can access information and gain entry into a range of sites relevant to the HR profession.

Teleworkers Web Site

http://www.telecentres.com

This site offers a directory of UK based teleworkers. It also includes some useful background information on teleworking.

Trades Union Congress (TUC)

http://www.tuc.org.uk/

The federation of the UK's trade unions. Its web site provides campaign information, briefing and a directory.

UNISON

http://www.unison.org.uk/

The biggest trade union in the UK, representing about 1.4 million public sector workers.

Online recruitment services

JobSearch UK
http://www.jobsearch.co.uk/
Here you can submit your CV or search for vacancies.

JobSite
http://www.jobsite.co.uk/
This one contains vacancies from many industries. It provides job listings by email and distributes CVs to recruitment agencies.

Monster Board UK
http://www.monster.co.uk/
A well-known and very breezily presented online recruitment centre for job-seekers and employers alike.

PeopleBank
http://www.peoplebank.com/
An international database of job-seekers, from a wide range of providers who can be matched instantly to employers requirements; requires registration.

TAPS (The Appointments Section)
http://taps.com
Another UK recruitment site where you can search and apply for a new position, create your own web resume, and be notified of new developments via email.

Index